WHEN RUPERT MURDOCH CAME TO TEA

A Memoir

DAVID NUNAN

When Rupert Murdoch Came to Tea: A Memoir

Edited by Dorothy E. Zemach. Cover design by DJ Rogers.

Published in the United States by Wayzgoose Press.

This is a work of non-fiction, based on the personal recollections of the author. Some personal names have been changed to protect people's privacy. Spellings and vocabulary are Australian English; a glossary of terms that may be unfamiliar to North Americans is provided at the back of the book.

CONTENTS

For Rebecca, who inspired this memoir

PREFACE

'So what was it like? Back there. Back then.' My daughter posed the question as I sat at the dining table in our Hong Kong apartment sifting through photos my sister had sent to me from Adelaide—photos from our childhood that turned up in a box in my mother's house after she died. My daughter had been raised in the bustle of a crowded Asian city. I was born and bred in a working-class mining community in the arid interior of Australia in the middle of the last century. The photos scattered on the dining—table presented her with images that were alien and inexplicable.

Because she was on her way back to the States, where she was an art student, I said, 'I'll write to you'. I imagined that the account might run to five or six thousand words. I ended up with ten pieces that threatened to run to seventy thousand words. They cover a period from the mid-1950s to the late 1960s.

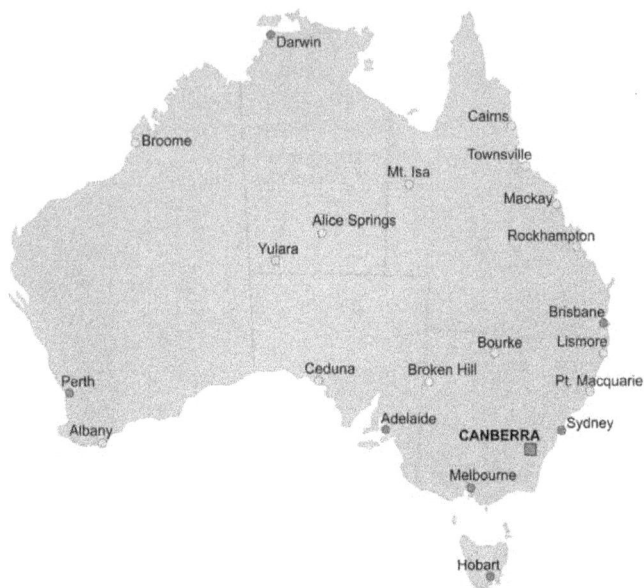

WHAT WAS IT LIKE?

Dear Bec,

Do you remember that day in late May? You'd collected the mail, and tossed a padded envelope onto my desk as I sat working. It contained a collection of photos that Marg had turned up at the back of a wardrobe as she was clearing out Grandma's things. We always knew she was a bit of a hoarder, but had no idea of the extent of her acquisitiveness. The amount of stuff she had secreted in the nooks and crannies of the house was heroic. Marg trashed a lot of it, but I was glad the photos had survived.

Later in the day, you looked through the photos and asked, 'What was it like?'

'What was what like?'

'Growing up there.'

'Where?'

'There', you persisted, pointing.

'Different!'

'Different?'

'Very different.'

'So how did you get from there to here?'

'There' was a mining community in the semi-arid interior of outback Australia. 'Here', Hong Kong, where you grew up, is a noisy, bustling Asian city, half a world and a whole generation away.

'What was it like?' Let me give you a snapshot of where I came from, and maybe you can work it out for yourself.

———

You had your first international trip, to the Middle East and Europe, before you were two, and by your eighth birthday had visited every continent on earth save one. At eight, I had barely been three hundred miles from my home. My world was ring-fenced by *The Gen*, or regeneration area, a swathe of land surrounding Broken Hill, which was referred to by the locals as 'The Hill' or 'The Barrier'—rarely 'Broken Hill'. *The Gen* had been planted with hardy shrubs in an attempt to curb the sand storms that blighted the town from time to time.

You've grown up with CD players, computers, cable television, and the products that spilled from the fertile imagination of Steve Jobs (may he rest in peace): iPods, iPhones, iPads, MacBooks, and goodness knows what else. Although television came to Australian cities in the 1950s, it didn't reach Broken Hill until the year after I had left. We were forced to find other forms of entertainment—not that it did us any harm.

'What was it like?' If you really want to know, read on. In these pieces, prompted by the photos scattered on my desktop, I have tried to capture what it was like for me. I started out to write a thirty- or forty-page account of growing up on the red dirt roads of a mining town west of the Darling River half a century ago.

But once I started, the writing took on a life of its own, and these pieces are the result. I'm not sure that I can give you a convincing explanation of how I got to what I am now from where I was then. Hopefully, however, these pieces will give you a partial answer at least to your question. The pictures may not be vibrant enough for you. I've used charcoals rather than the oils that you're used to.

I've written the pieces roughly in chronological order, from my early childhood to late adolescence. If you asked any of the other 42,000 inhabitants of The Hill for their recollections, you'd get a very different set of stories. If, in another time and place, I recalled these stories, no doubt they'd look very different too. That's the way of memory. It speaks with a different tongue at different times.

I named the collection after the title of the second piece in order to get your attention. I know bits of you pretty well, although there are other parts that I will never know. That's the way it is with fathers and daughters, I'm told. If I'd called the collection *Fragments from my Early Life* or something similar, I know for a fact that you'd never have picked it up. *Broken Hill in a Nutshell* would have been the kiss of death.

This is unfortunate, but it's a fact of life. When, in late adolescence, I went to Sydney, or 'The Big Smoke' as it was called by people from the bush, to take the first step on the road that led me here, people would occasionally ask me where I was from. The response 'Broken Hill' evoked a range of emotions. Words were unnecessary. You could see it in their faces as they backed away.

Almost a decade later, in England, the confession 'I'm from Australia' sometimes evoked a similar reaction. The uncertainty in their eyes. 'Am I about to be bashed?' 'My God! He's going to vomit on me.' I guess it's human nature not to let cosmic ignorance come between attitudes, opinions, and beliefs.

But you never experienced that. You were never recognizably Australian, were you? I doubt that you even see yourself as a creature of the Antipodes. Your accent never gave you away, nor your blonde hair and blue eyes. You might just as well have been from Norway, or Sweden, like Alex, your blonde, blue-eyed double, as from New South Wales. As a freshman, sophomore, and senior in the back blocks of Massachusetts, you were recognizably different, but in an exotic way, like your black friend from Harlem— the one we met creating a fresco on the wall of the basket-ball court outside the art barn that sunny afternoon in early Fall.

I doubt you even remember that afternoon, and if you do, I bet it seems an age away. For me it seems like yesterday. I can still smell the late summer grass, still see the turning leaves, remember smiling in an unfocused fatherly way as you hugged your friends returning from summer, like you, for their second year of uncertainty and challenge.

When, from time to time, people ask me where I'm from, I take delight in their confusion when I announce that I'm from Broken Hill.

'Broken Hill?'

'Broken Hill! I guess you've never heard of it.'

A puzzled shake of the head.

'Ever heard of BHP Billiton?'

'Indeed. I have shares in the company. The largest resource company in the world.'

'Well, just so you know, BHP stands for Broken Hill Proprietary. The richest resource company in the world was born on the same square of earth as me.'

———

Such a shame, the ignorance from outside, and the decline from within. Broken Hill was a place rich in ore until the ore was stripped away by the mining companies, who then left it for dead. It was then, and remains today, a place rich in characters and local history. Some of these were home-grown. Others were attracted by the prospect of work or by the town's reputation:

- Willie, the Belgian mercenary who learned how to kill people in the Congo and who sold me my first (and last) handgun—a Webley .38—arrived a bitter and twisted man. Broken Hill taught him how to reconnect with the human race.
- Pro Hart, the miner made good as an artist, whose paintings now hang in Buckingham Palace of all places, and who is now the richest man in the Broken Hill cemetery. His mining mates dubbed him 'Pro' or 'Professor', not because he had any formal education, which he didn't, but because he was a Clever Dick and extremely eccentric to boot. In addition to painting, he invented machine guns and built organs.
- June Bronhill, born Gough, who changed her

name in tribute to the town that raised money to send her to England to hone her magnificent voice. 'Our Junie' became one of Australia's most celebrated singers, starring at the Sadler's Wells Opera Company, in London's West End theatres, and on the screen. But she never lost the common touch. On a visit back to the Hill, so my father once told me, she attended a local football match. The crowd gave her a cheer. She gave them the bird.

Back to Rupert Murdoch. Yes, he came to town. And he came to tea. I don't know if you remember Grandma's teas; probably not, but they were good. You used to love her pumpkin scones with clotted cream and strawberry jam. She made them for Rupert, along with chicken and shredded lettuce sandwiches. There would have been cake as well, her rich fruitcake, lurking in the kitchen to be called upon if needed. I don't remember the fruitcake, but I'm sure it was there.

But Rupert Murdoch was only one of many celebrities and scoundrels who came and went, or came and stayed, or entered life in Broken Hill and later ran away for good. While I kick off these stories with my recollection, such as it is, of the evening that the media-mogul-to-be came for tea, most of the other stories are about people I knew, grew up with, loved, feared, and loathed.

As I began to write, long-forgotten characters and incidents began to re-emerge. Some of the people in these pieces you've met, of course—siblings, cousins, uncles and aunts. At one stage, I thought of including photos. I have one of you and Elva. That would have been a cool one to include, because at 90-plus years of age she is the last living member of her generation, and you are the youngest of yours. She actually features in the Murdoch story, as well as in the one that follows, when I talk about how she and Don saved my life.

As far as possible, I've tried to be truthful and factual; although as you get older, you'll find that fact and fiction, truth and falsity don't inhabit different universes. I was about to say, they co-exist within us as we journey through life, but I'm uncomfortable with the metaphor, or cliché rather, of life as a journey. A fiction, but a persistent one. *Bernice and Trevor are pleased to announce the arrival of Baby Amelia*. Amelia didn't arrive from anywhere—she isn't a train, for goodness' sake. She was getting a free ride inside Bernice. *Tony Celotto went to glory*. He didn't go anywhere. He just died. And instantly as well, when his utility truck flipped over on the Silverton Road. I went to his funeral. Viewed him in the open casket. My first real-life dead body. So, fictionalizing fact is woven into the very fabric of language.

It's unseasonably cold right here right now. The winter winds have reached all the way from Mongolia to the South China Sea. But not as cold as where you are in the middle of Massachusetts, I'm sure. I got your email, by the way, and will transfer the school fees as soon as I can get to the bank. I can't do it online—the amount exceeds my daily limit by a long shot.

Anyway, I digress. 'Get on with it', I hear you say. So I will.

———

In the pages that follow, where necessary, I have disguised details and changed some names. This is to protect myself as much as the characters in these accounts. I hope that you can see the accounts for what it they are: subjective snapshots of life in a tough but surprisingly tender Australian mining town, as seen through the eyes of a kid who didn't know it then, but who came to appreciate how lucky he was to have grown up there. And I hope it answers your question: 'What was it like, Dad?'

Here's a bit of history. Please don't skip it, OK? Promise?

The low line of ranges that would one day form a backdrop to the city of Broken Hill was discovered in 1890 by a young boundary rider called Charles Rasp. Charles Rasp was well known to us as schoolboys. This had less to do with the pivotal role he played in the founding of the town than with the fact that his name (given a slight phonological stretch) rhymes with 'arse'. This provided a seam of a somewhat different kind—limericks, schoolboy doggerel, and so on. Most of these have, thankfully, disappeared. The following is an example of how his name, to my generation at least, was memorialised:

> *A young boundary rider named Rasp*
> *Had an unenviable task:*
> *To keep his flash rocks*
> *Away from the cops*
> *He shoved them right up his arse.*

Once, I started to tell you about this German boundary rider called Rasp, and you interrupted immediately. You've probably forgotten the conversation, but here it is, as best as I can recall.

'What's a boundary rider?' you asked.

'Well, you're good at languages,' I replied. 'You speak at least three that I know of—you figure it out.'

'Just tell me.'

'A boundary rider is someone who rides boundaries. Your grandfather started out as a boundary rider. He left school at the age of eleven and took a job as a boundary rider in order to help support the family—he had six siblings who made it to adulthood. He had a horse, a rifle, water-bags, and a pack containing sugar, salt, flour, and tea. That was about it, along with a bedroll that was slung across the horse's rump. His job was to ride the fences that kept the sheep belonging to his boss on their side of the fence, and the sheep belonging to the adjoining property on their side of the fence. Whenever he came to a break in the fence, he would dismount, tether the horse, and repair the fence. Then he'd ride on.'

'That sounds like a shit job.'

'It was a job. The first time around, it took him two weeks. In all that time, he didn't see a single person. It's no surprise that many young boundary riders became very fond of sheep. He survived by shooting rabbits and the occasional kangaroo. With the 'roos, he'd cut out the fillet and leave the rest of the carcass to the scavengers. That's what he lived on—whatever game he could shoot, and damper.'

'Damper?'

'Made from flour, salt, and water. At the end of the two-week ride, he returned to the homestead exhausted with a footsore horse, and his boss gave him his pay, a shilling, and a packet of cigarettes—10 Craven A cork-tipped cigarettes.'

"'Is that all?" asked Granddad. The boss thought he'd done a pretty good job to get back in one piece, so he gave him a pat on the back and a box of matches as a bonus.'

So—back to the history lesson. And I hope you're still reading. I know you're not crazy about geology, but you like history, so hopefully you'll find it relatively painless. It's important for you to know this stuff so that the stories to come make sense.

At some distant point in the geological past, a shift in the plates that make up the earth's crust thrust a lode-bearing seam of ore through the surface of the earth. The line of load arched like a massive metallic coat hanger, the top of the arch presenting itself as a low range of weathered hills that happened to contain the largest deposits of silver, lead, and zinc in the world.

Forty years before your grandfather roamed those ancient hills, Charles Rasp, the boundary rider, would spend two to three weeks at a time alone in the outback, riding the fences that separated one property from another, repairing breaks in the wire and replacing uprooted fence posts. At night he would spread out his bedroll, light a fire, make damper and tea, and look at the stars.

On one particular day Rasp was picking his way on horseback through the rocky outcrop that is now known as The Hill. At one point, he dismounted and led his horse over a low range. He was a long way from the homestead and didn't want his horse to throw a shoe. For no reason in particular, he stopped and began to examine the shards of rock at his feet. Unlike the dun-coloured rocks further north, they shimmered and glittered in the sun. Some were shot through with metallic lumps that had a golden sheen.

'Fool's gold', he thought. Nevertheless, he put several samples into his saddlebag and pushed on.

Much later, back at the homestead, he showed the rock samples to his boss—and the rest, as they say, is history. One company, the Broken Hill Proprietary Company, born on this unpromising outcrop in the middle of nowhere, was destined to become (and remain) Australia's largest and richest resource company. Although BHP severed its connection with the town in the early days of its development, it retained the name, and 'Broken Hill' became synonymous with mineral wealth around the world—except, as I've already said, not many people make the connection these days.

At first, the riches were there for the taking. All you had to do was scratch the surface of the earth. The scratches got deeper and deeper, turning into open-cut mines. Eventually these deep scars in the earth gave way to underground mines. Some of these were destined to be among the deepest in the world as they followed the line of lode in a descending arc deep into the bowels of the earth. The various mines either faltered or merged until, when I was a boy, there were only four main players in the game: the Zinc Mine, New Broken Hill Consolidated, the South, and the North.

Uncle Don was underground manager of the South Mine. He was a great innovator and oversaw the task of linking the South and North mines through an underground tunnel, something that was considered a mining triumph in its day. I owe my life to Don, as you'll discover if you read on, and he and Elva sat with you as you struggled for life as a six-year-old with acute rheumatoid arthritis. So they form an important connection between the past, the present, and the future. It was sad when Don died last year—a connection unplugged—but Elva is forging strongly into her nineties. I visited her when I was in Sydney last, and she wanted to know all about you and Jenny and your doings.

Well, back to the history, such as it is. I hope you're still with me.

One day, despite the efforts of Don and his colleagues, the line of lode simply petered out. The ends of the coat hanger were reached. The mining companies spent a fortune in diamond drilling operations to find the continuation of the line of lode, but they never did, and the town went into a long, slow decline that's still going on. Occasional injections of money from the movie industry (the *Mad Max* movies, among others, were shot there) and tourism provided only temporary relief from the malaise.

So this is where I grew up, and this is a story about what it was like to grow up in a mining city in the middle of the Australian bush in the middle of the 20th century.

Whoever coined the phrase 'the middle of nowhere' must have had Broken Hill in mind, because that's where it was—and still is, although the Road to Nowhere is now all-weather tarmac. Seven hundred miles due west of Sydney. Three hundred and thirty miles northeast of Adelaide. It sprawls about the low range of lode-bearing hills; and, when I was a child, it was dominated by the artificial mountains of skimp, grey silt-like stuff that was left over once the ore was extracted from the mines. Most of the skimp dumps are gone now, reprocessed when extraction techniques for the ore they still contained were improved. To me the town is all the poorer for their demise.

WHEN RUPERT MURDOCH CAME TO TEA

Little Paul spoke first. 'Why do we have to go to our room?'

'Because I told you to.' A common parental response, back then.

'But why?'

'Because Dad is bringing a really important person home.'

'Why?' It was his word of the month, and he was determined to do it to death.

'Why what?'

Little Paul blinked at Mum through his glasses. 'Why is he important?'

'He's your Father's boss.'

'Oh.' Little Paul gave her a solemn look, as though the response made perfect sense to him.

'He owns the paper. In fact, he has two: one here and one in Adelaide.'

She turned to the baby who was squatting on the floor. 'Stop picking your nose! And you two get to your room like I told you to.'

———

I wasn't sure why having two newspapers made our Dad's boss so important that we had to be sent to our rooms. We had two newspapers too: the one our Dad worked for and the Union newspaper. Everyone in town got the Union newspaper, whether they wanted it or not. It came free with your Union membership. The Union newspaper was printed overnight and arrived on the doorstep in the morning. Occasionally, it arrived before people left for work or school, but more often than not it spent the day in the front yard yellowing in the sun and being peed on by passing dogs. The evening newspaper, the one our Dad worked for, was printed during the day and delivered in the evening.

Our Mum was nervous. She made us put on our best clothes: the ones she spent hours labouring over, cutting out the fabric from a pattern, assembling shirts, shorts, and skirts on a foot operated sewing machine, then folding them in tissue paper and putting them in the 'only to be opened for births and birthdays' drawer. (Funerals were added later, when we were old enough to deal with the idea of death.) She always made our clothes several sizes too big —'So you can grow into them.' We grew as the clothes languished in the drawer, and often only got to wear them once or twice before nature dictated that they be handed on to younger siblings, relatives, or ragged neighbours.

There was a rumble of voices and the clinking of glasses. I looked through a chink in the door, but could only see the edge of the upholstered lounge and a shoe that jiggled up and down on the end of a foot. It was an interesting shoe. A type I'd never seem before. Firstly, it was black. At the time, the only person I knew who wore black shoes was our local doctor. Uncle Don had black steel-capped boots that were too heavy to lift, but that was because he worked on the mine. After work he changed into an old brown pair.

The second interesting thing about the shoes was the strange pattern in the leather. Some years later, my Dad acquired a pair—brown, of course—and I learned a new word: brogues. Those shoes remained one of his proudest possessions for the rest of his life. When Paul got married, at the tender age of seventeen, Dad lent him the brogues to save him the embarrassment of getting hitched in a pair of scuffed loafers.

It was boring in the bedroom. I drew a picture, but it was no good, so I tore it up. Little Paul whined in the background. 'Why do we have to be in our room?' I told him to shut up. He lay down on his bed and went to sleep, drool seeping out of his mouth and down his cheek.

Then Mum came into the room. She grabbed Paul's ankle and shook it. When he opened his eyes, she licked a finger and swiped the drool off his cheek. She licked it again and smoothed down the hair on the back of my head.

Later, she would fix our hair problems with Brylcreem. Brylcreem was all the rage among the big kids—essential for keeping their Elvis cuts in place. The local commercial radio station used to play the Brylcreem jingle nonstop:

> Brylcreem, a little dab'll do ya!
> Use more, only if ya dare
> But watch out
> The gals will all pursue ya,
> They'll love to put their fingers through
>   your hair.

When we'd been spruced up to Mum's satisfaction, she marched us into the lounge room to meet our Dad's boss. Dad and the stranger were sitting on the newly recovered sofa drinking beer. An untouched plate of sandwiches rested on an occasional table that stood between them.

Although he was shorter than Dad, he filled the room. He wore a suit and tie, and it wasn't even Sunday. Dad also wore a tie. Although he had a suit, he wasn't wearing it. Instead he had on his best cardigan, the one with the leather patches on the elbows. I remember most clearly his boss's slicked-back black hair, his eyebrows and his plump cheeks. But most of all I remember his eyes. As we were introduced, he nodded but didn't speak. When it was my turn, his brows came together, and his eyes went clean through me to the floorboards. I would like to say that it was a look of dislike—disdain, even—but it wasn't. It was a look of complete indifference.

On a chair set at right angles to the other two men was Doc Jolly, the Managing Editor of the newspaper. I was yet to learn about nicknames, and thought that he was a real doctor. It seemed odd that a doctor would work for a newspaper, but then he was an adult, and adults had unfathomable ways. He was a bachelor and lived alone in a boarding house in Oxide Street. Sometimes Dad would bring him home unannounced from the club for Sunday lunch. That would throw Mum into a flap, although she kept her mouth shut until after he had gone. Then she would mutter under her breath, 'I know he's your boss, but I don't know why you have to bring that old dipso home.' She would utter the words with resignation, knowing full well that nothing she ever said cut any ice with Dad.

As we grew older, we learned that Dad, tough as leather

and hard as nails, had tremendous admiration and respect bordering on hero worship for young Rupert; as, indeed, he'd had for Rupert's father, Sir Keith. He always maintained that the older Murdoch had been done in by the forces of evil, victim of a conspiracy that had robbed him of his newspaper empire. When he died, he had pitifully little to leave to his son, and Rupert, returning at the age of twenty-two from Oxford University, had to begin almost from scratch. 'He's going to change the face of publishing,' Dad said. 'You just wait and see.' We waited, and we saw, and he did.

———

Dad had a few publishing firsts of his own. *The Barrier Miner* was printed on an old Goss press that was as big as a house. Barring mechanical failure, the paper went to press at 3.30 every weekday and twice on Saturday, once for the regular edition and later for the sports edition. When he had checked that everything was in order, Dad would pull a greasy rag from the back pocket of his overalls, wipe his hands, and nod to one of the apprentices who had the honour of hitting the big red button on the side of the press with the palm of his hand. I will never forget the thrill of being lifted up by the armpits to start the machine myself on one or two occasions.

The press turned over slowly at first, cogs and wheels nudged into life electronically, groaning, creaking, and complaining. Then it gathered speed and began to spit out papers that were shovelled up by the apprentices and passed over a counter into the packing room where they were counted, bundled up, and passed out on to the footpath.

Here delivery boys rolled them up, shovelled them into leather panniers, and rode off on their delivery rounds.

Once it was running at full speed, the huge mechanical beast was awesome—frightening almost. And the noise, the heat, and the smell of grease were overpowering. It was like standing next to a huge steam locomotive that was bolted to the ground. The whole building shook. Speech was impossible. Dad loved it. He stood there wiping his face, smiling at the beast. It wasn't easy to make him smile, but the beast managed it every day. He lost three kilos in weight every afternoon, and then went to Mario's pub and promptly put it back on. (Mario and his pub were subsequently to have their fifteen seconds of fame in the film *Priscilla, Queen of the Desert*.)

Dad was very proud of that Goss printing press over which he presided. When it broke down, the pain on his face was palpable. It was though he had been injured himself. He would stay in the printing room, sometimes through the night, until the press was once more in good working order.

When it came to printing presses, our Dad knew his stuff. Now and then the telephone would ring in the small hours of the morning. Dad would wash his face, comb his hair, get on his bicycle, and ride off into the night to repair the opposition's printing press.

Once a year, the head mechanic from News Limited in Adelaide arrived to help Dad strip down the Goss press, clean it, and reassemble it. They worked right through the weekend, starting as soon as the final edition was printed on Saturday night and finishing as dawn broke on Monday morning. Aided and abetted by her sister, who had a car, Mum ferried supplies to the front line troops: Cornish pasties, ox tongue sandwiches, and thermos flasks of tea. One Sunday morning, I was once permitted to go with them and was astonished to see the mighty Goss machine reduced to mounds of metallic rubble surrounded by puddles of oil.

One year, Rupert Murdoch decreed that a colour advertising supplement was to be inserted into all of his provincial newspapers. By this stage he had a string of such newspapers across the country. In those days, supplements had to be inserted into each newspaper by hand. Dad got me to recruit my school friends, and we would descend on the *Barrier Miner* office after school to earn pocket money for doing a tedious and tiring job. The problem with this procedure was that it held up delivery of the newspaper to the customers. Delivery boys who worked the pubs, and who were used to generous tips, got a clip over the ears instead.

So our Dad figured out how to insert the colour supplement into the newspaper mechanically. When each issue rolled off the press, it already contained the insert. When news of this feat reached head office in Adelaide, Dad became a bit of a celebrity. He was even interviewed, and had his photo in the *Adelaide News*. No-one ever figured out how he did it, and he took his secret with him to the grave. He enjoyed his little secret, and his fifteen minutes of fame.

———

On the night our Dad brought Rupert Murdoch home, we sat awestruck by his fearsome presence. We had no idea that something momentous was about to occur, something that would mythologise Rupert in the eyes of the townspeople.

After they had consumed several bottles of beer, the three men rose, as though through some prearranged signal. Dad guided Rupert Murdoch by the elbow out of the front door and into Doc Jolly's car, which stood under a gum tree on the edge of the road. We hovered on the verandah and watched them go. Then we were allowed to have our tea, as the evening meal was called.

'Where are they going?' asked Paul.

'Out', said Mum.

'Out where?' He was always asking questions.

'Eat your food', said Mum distributing the sandwiches that the men had left untouched.

They were going to the Two-up School. Short of betting on two flies crawling up a wall, two-up is the most primitive form of gambling there is. A spinner places two pennies on a short wooden spatula and spins the pennies into the air. Punters standing around the spinner bet on whether the pennies would land heads up ('Two 'e heads') or tails up ('Two 'e tails'). If one penny lands heads up and the other lands tails up, the spinner throws the coins again. If you want sight of the very Two-up School that Rupert visited, watch the iconic Australian movie *Wake in Fright*, set in Broken Hill and featuring the Two-up School, a drunken Donald Pleasance, and a youthful Jack Thompson in his first major movie role. If you look carefully, you might also see my right elbow pulling the arm of a poker machine in the Returned Services League scene—I was on vacation from university when the film was made and was lucky enough to land a job as an extra.

Statisticians will tell you that each throw of the coins is

independent of the one that went before, and that with every toss of the coins, there is an equal chance of the coins coming down heads or tails. However, many punters believed in the power of serial betting. They would wait until there had been a run of three straight heads or three straight tails and then bet the other way.

In the rest of the country, two-up was a mild form of entertainment for inebriated ex-servicemen after the annual Anzac Day march. For punters in Broken Hill, it was a ritual. The Two-up School was open until the early hours of the morning seven days a week. More or less. It closed for several hours once when the State Governor made an official visit, as did the pubs, which generally opened and shut at the whim of the publican.

It would be many years before I made my first visit to the Two-up School, and it's many years now since I made my last, but I remember it well. To get in, you had to go down a back alley that ran parallel to Agent Street, the main street in town. Halfway along the alley, there was a modest hamburger joint. They made good hamburgers and did a roaring trade late at night. There's nothing like a greasy hamburger to soak up an excess of alcohol.

If you kept your eyes open as you munched on your burger, you'd notice a steady stream of customers ignoring the reedy man in a grimy apron who took the food orders. They would head past the counter towards a door at the rear of the hamburger bar that was guarded by two large men with crooked noses and no necks. There they would pause to be inspected. If the guards liked what they saw, they would admit the visitor with a faint nod of the head. Occasionally, a particularly inebriated customer would be turned away with a wave of the hand.

In our mid-teens, on a Friday night after an illegal drink or two, my friends and I took to finishing the night with a hamburger at the Two-up School. One night, as we're devouring hamburgers and watching the punters come and go, Pete Fielding, who knows all about the Two-up School from his two big brothers, both avid gamblers says, 'I always wanted to have a look in there, particularly on payday. Some blokes blow their entire pay packet for the fortnight in a couple of hours. Then they have to go home and explain themselves to the Missus.'

'Let's go in and have a look', says Russ Carney.

'Oh, those goons'd never let us through the door', says Pete.

'I'm gunna give it a go', says Russ, who's game for anything. He finishes his burger and strolls over to the two goons on the door. Pete and I stare in astonishment as the larger of the two men steps aside and Russ passes through the door.

'Jeez, look at that, would ya?' says Pete. 'Come on.'

We present ourselves to the neckless doorman who'd let Russ in. He looks at us for a nanosecond and says, 'Fuck off', in a low voice. We turn tail and slink out into the alley-way. It's only later we learn that the guard on the door that night is Russ's mum's second cousin once removed—almost family, really.

The following Friday night, the three of us meet up again in the back bar of the Caledonian Hotel. We wouldn't last five seconds in the front bar, but they're very relaxed about underage drinking out the back. Russ says that if we shout his drinks, then he'll see if his second cousin once removed will let us in. Pete drinks beer. Neither Russ nor I like the bitterness of West End beer, brewed specially for the Broken Hill palate. Russ drinks rum and Coke. I drink scotch and dry. These poofter-drinks, as Pete calls them, don't leave you reeking of alcohol, a distinct advantage in my case, as my mum has the nose of a bloodhound when it comes to alcohol and cigarettes.

At the Two-up School, we front Russ's goon cousin and his cousin's goon mate. Russ is fine. Pete, fortified by three middies of West End is, fine. For some reason, I have butterflies in my stomach. Russ's cousin looks us over and nods.

Past the men with broken noses is the School itself. It's nothing fancy ; a frenzied huddle of men around the spinner and a couple of men who run the School. You call your bet —heads or tails—pair up with someone in the huddle who has called a different tune, wait for the spinning coins to arc into the air, and then settle your bets. It's amazing how dramatic a series of simple human actions can be.

Once accustomed to the excitement and the drama, Pete decides to have a go. He pulls a dollar note from his pocket and, as the spinner is setting the coins on his spatula and calls 'Two 'e heads'. A little man on the other side of the ring nods. The coins go spinning into the air and land on the mat. One of the men who is running the show rushes over and bends over the coins. 'Tails', he calls.

'Fuck it', says Pete and passes his dollar to the little man in the felt hat on the other side of the ring.

———

On the night in question, I woke in the dead of night to the creak of a floorboard. I lay in bed, frozen with fear, eyes screwed tightly shut, wondering if it was the ghost that occasionally stalked the house at night or just a parent making their way to the lean-to toilet at the back of the yard.

The floorboards always creaked at night. Dad tried to stop this with hammer, nails, and sheets of Masonite that he laid between the floorboards and the Feltex that covered them. However, this solution failed, like others he tried. The creaking boards were part of the personality of the house. You couldn't get in or out of the house without the floorboards giving you away. Sometimes they would give a ghostly squeak of their own accord. As teenagers this became a problem, one that I solved by staying home. Paul solved it by removing the mosquito screen from the bedroom window.

The floorboards squeaked and groaned again. I looked through a crack in the bedroom door. Dad was at the far end of the sitting room. He was bent over the dining table embracing a crystal bowl containing an arrangement of dried flowers. The boards squeaked again. Mum appeared, shook him on the shoulder, and said 'Go to bed'.

Next day was Sunday. We kids went to church. It was the anniversary of grandmother's death. Mother gave me a dollar for the collection plate.

We were Catholics because she was. She was fierce in her determination that we go to Sunday Mass, but she never went herself. The only time I ever saw her cross the threshold of the little suburban church was on the day of my First Communion when she turned up with a tray of sausage rolls for the post-service feast.

I gave the note to Father Leonard and asked him to remember Grandmother in his prayers. I felt important when, at a certain point in the service, he said, 'Today we pray for the soul of Lillian Viola Price'. Billy O'Dowd kicked me in the leg and snickered. Like the rest of us, he was there on the orders of his parents. Unlike the rest of us, his parents sat square-shouldered and attentive in the front pew.

By the time we got home from church, Dad was at the Musicians' Club—the Musos. Mum, as usual, was baking a leg of lamb and roasting potatoes. The Sunday ritual. It was my job to pick some of the mint leaves that grew profusely out the back under the garden tap that wouldn't stop dripping. I took them inside and made mint sauce. Later I graduated to gravy, learning just how much flour to sprinkle on the meat juices and fat, and how much water to add so the gravy was thick, the way Dad liked. I was famished, so I stuffed some mint leaves in my mouth. Paul was lying on his back drumming his legs on the floor and calling for his lunch. But we were not allowed to eat until Dad came home, which eventually he did, unsteadily on his bike, then washed his hands and sat at the head of the table to carve the lamb. We had to eat all of our vegetables first. Then we were allowed to eat the meat. And we had to leave something on our plate.

'Always leave the table feeling like you could eat some more', Dad used to say. Well, that wasn't difficult. 'And don't put your elbows on the table.' These were the two rules that had to be obeyed. A third rule, 'Don't speak unless you're spoken to' went by the board pretty early on. When we were children, our parents couldn't shut us up. When we were teenagers, they had a job getting us to open our mouths. We would sit through the evening meal in surly silence, while they did their best to cajole a word out of us.

The stock response to 'How was school today?' was 'Same as yesterday'.

In the middle of the afternoon, Dad's younger brother Jimmy turns up. He and Dad sit at the kitchen table. I sit on the old lounge pushed up against one wall and pretend to read a comic book.

Dad opens a bottle of a beer. 'Bit early, but it is Sunday', he says, overlooking the fact that it isn't his first for the day.

'If you're thirsty, you have a drink', says Jimmy. 'Good luck!'—the common way of toasting in Broken Hill. 'Cheers!' was considered totally effete.

'Good luck!' They drain their glasses, and Jimmy pushes his across the table for a refill.

'That boss of yours won't be getting invited back to the Two-up School any time soon', he says.

'Suppose not', said Dad. 'That Rupert. Have to hand it to him, eh?'

Hiding behind my magazine, I learn that Rupert Murdoch had done what no one else had ever done before: He had broken the bank. Skinned the place. Cleaned out everyone.

'You've never seen anything like it', says Dad. 'He's got the Midas touch, all right.' And then, as hardened miners began to drift out of the room, empty pay packets in hand, he called them back and shelled out wads of the money he'd won so that they could go on playing.

'To him it was just a game. It was lucky he didn't get lynched. Only Rupert Murdoch could have got away with it.' According to Dad, only Rupert Murdoch would have had the gall and the balls. And the cash.

At the tender age of seven, I had only the vaguest idea of what two-up was all about. I knew it was a form of gambling, and I knew about gambling. I knew that very often it made people either very angry or very sad. Sometimes they were both angry and sad at the same time. Then on other, rarer occasions, it made them very happy.

My grandmother on Mum's side, the sainted Lillian Viola, was a great gambler, although she didn't call it gambling. She called it having a flutter on the horses, or the dogs, or the Friday night trots. Saturday afternoons she spent with her ear glued to the wireless. Her other daughter, who happened to be Uncle Jimmy's wife as well as Mum's sister, would place bets for her with the bookie who ran an illegal gambling operation out of the back bar of the Hillside Hotel. Now and then Cousin Pete and I would go with her and sit in the car drinking lemonade while she completed gambling transactions for her mother.

In the 1960s Rupert Murdoch made good on Dad's promise. He announced the birth of a national daily newspaper called *The Australian*. It was to be a broadsheet, not a tabloid, and would appear simultaneously in all state capitals. 'How could this be?' wondered people who knew the inner workings of the newspaper world. Dad knew. Multiple trays of linotype would be set in Canberra and air-freighted out to each state capital for printing.

Thanks to the Internet, these days the simultaneous publishing of national and, indeed, international newspapers and journals is a piece of cake. However, back in the 60s it was a considerable achievement. Many people predicted that *The Australian* would be short-lived. However, it prospered and is going strong to this day, although it has never made money. Somehow it retains a spot in a part of Rupert's anatomy that some people deny exists. The newspaper was intended to counter Murdoch's image as the printer of low-end tabloids, to establish him as a publisher of quality, and to provide him with a platform through which he could wield political influence.

These days, when you observe the right-wing anti-intellectual diatribes spewing from Murdoch's global Fox network, it's difficult to believe that he was once a bit of a lefty. In league with the genuinely left-wing Rohan Rivett, editor of *The Adelaide News*, he championed causes such as pillorying the gerrymandering right-wing State government and overturning the murder conviction of a simple-minded aborigine. The latter cause resulted in the newspaper being charged with seditious libel, which in those days was just short of treason.

When Dad bought his pair of Murdoch lookalike brogues, our mother gave him a reproachful look, but said nothing. She rarely did, expressing her disapproval through pursed lips and silence. Because they were expensive, they mainly lived in the box they had come home in. On Sunday mornings, Dad would sit on the back step and give them a good spit and polish. He'd turn them this way and that, admiring their sheen, before returning them to their box. I can only remember seeing him wear them twice: one time to Cousin Robert's wedding at the Golf Club, the other to Uncle Doc's funeral after he got electrocuted or died from overdoing the Bundaberg Rum. He wasn't really our uncle, but that's what we called our Dad's drinking mates. We had two Uncle Docs, neither of whom were doctors, the one who overdid the Bundy Rum and the one who was Dad's boss. It was all kind of confusing.

———

Years later, I'm living as a graduate student in England. This 'green and pleasant land' is suffering its worst drought in centuries. The landscape is brown and withered. I'm stricken down with what the doctors say is a life-threatening condition and require emergency surgery. My parents, pensioners who can ill afford it, fly over from Australia. They've never been out of the country. Even within Australia, they've been to very few places. During the Great Depression, my father rode his bicycle to Tasmania in search of work, but that was about as far as he'd ever been. Now and then he'd wax lyrical about Tassie and promise to take our mother there, but he never got around to it.

Before my parents arrive in England, I undergo emergency surgery. However, due to the wonders of the National Health Service and modern surgical techniques, I recover in time to pick them up at Heathrow. I then have the opportunity to experience the country through other eyes.

Dad has the eye of an engineer. Had he not left school at the age of eleven to help support the family, I'm sure he'd have become one. He marvels at the old buildings, particularly the gothic cathedrals. 'How did they do it?' he asks in wonder, craning his neck towards flying buttresses, soaring arches, and spectacular stained glass windows. When in Wells Cathedral, he is asked by the verger to remove the woollen cap he has taken to wearing to ward off the chill that can suddenly descend, even in summer, I brace myself for his ire and am surprised when he meekly complies.

The day after they arrive in London, my mother succumbs to jetlag just as we are about to go for lunch at a local pub. We leave her snoring gently on the sofa and go down the road for a ploughman's and a pint. As we leave the flat, we bump into my upstairs neighbour, a young German woman called Gerta. She and Dad take a shine to each other. He refers to her, embarrassingly, as 'the New Australian lass upstairs.' Dad will eventually go to his grave steadfast in the belief that he is the only person on the face of the earth who doesn't have an accent. Everyone else is either a 'New Australian' or a 'Pom'.

Prior to his visit to England, Dad had a low opinion of the English, seeing them as unionists and trouble-makers. However, over a pint of lager (he tries real ale, pronounces it 'dishwater' and, for the rest of the trip, sticks steadfastly to Carling Black Label lager) he confesses that he has changed his view. 'Marvellous country!' he pronounces after a pint or two. 'Marvellous people!' Even the immigration officer had shaken him by the hand and said 'Welcome!' He ducks his head in wonder at the fact that there are no Poms in England. They've all migrated to Australia.

Settling in to his second pint, his thoughts turn to Rupert. 'Sent me a message when I retired', he says. 'Fancy that!' He ruminates, and then: 'I had lunch with him in Sydney the day before we flew out. Always knew where you were with Rupert. Either he liked you or he didn't. Or he liked you and then changed his mind. If he did that, you found out soon enough. Like Red Rohan. Bit of a Commie, but Rupert made him Editor in Chief of *The News*. They were great pals for a while, but then they had a falling out and that was the end of Red Rohan.' Another ruminative pause. Another healthy draught of lager. 'Rupert told me that he had a newspaper here in the U.K.'

Dad decides that a third pint 'for the road' would be entirely appropriate. 'We don't want to go home too soon and disturb your mother.'

He also decides that he'd like to see a copy of Murdoch's

English newspaper, *The Sun*. This is Rupert's first foray into international publishing. 'I told you that he'd change the face of publishing', he says.

I wasn't sure that the purchase of a respectable mid-market broadsheet and the turning of it into a British scandal rag by an Antipodean newspaper proprietor could be characterised as 'changing the face of publishing', although the newspaper buying public seemed to agree. Daily sales shot into the millions, and remained that way, although the recent phone-tapping scandal changed all that.

Later, he acquired *The Times of London* from Lord Thomson of Fleet, and did begin revolutionizing newsprint publishing by breaking the British printing unions (a considerable feat in itself) and moving the production of newspapers into the digital age.

Another Canadian publisher with whom Rupert (dubbed The Dirty Digger by the British snobocracy) had something in common was Conrad Black. Both traded their citizenship, but for very different reasons. The Dirty Digger traded his Australian nationality for U.S. citizenship, which allowed him to buy into the film and television industry in North America. Not to be outdone by his compatriot, Lord Thomson of Fleet, Black exchanged his Canadian citizenship to become British, which subsequently enabled him to buy a seat in the British House of Lords—something that, for some strange reason, had been a lifelong dream.

But on this pallid afternoon, as England struggles into early summer, and as Dad and I sit in a dingy London pub drinking pints and eating cheese, chutney, bread, and pickled onions, Rupert the Hero is still very much an

Aussie. Dad buys a round for the road and I slip out to the newsstand for a copy of *The Sun*.

When I return, Dad is well into his pint. 'Not a patch on West End', he says. 'Not cold enough. Not enough gas. I told the barman. Nice young chap, but he didn't seem to know what I was talking about. I asked him how often they cleaned their pipes. Said he had no idea.'

'Here's your paper.'

He takes it and scans the front page with a printer's eye. Checks the alignment of the margins, the evenness of the print. He turns the page and is confronted by the Page Three Girl. His eyeballs almost meet, and he studies the picture as though looking for some sort of clue. None presents itself, so he proceeds slowly through the newspaper, scanning the headlines and accompanying photos.

Actress Beauty Bares All for Charity
  Mum Denies Murdering Son
    Rapist Fears: 16 Year Old Schoolgirl Found Dead
    Bigamist Tells How
    Nudists in Court for Naked Gardening

When he gets to the sports section, he gives up. The bulk of the section is given over to soccer, a game of which he has little knowledge and even less regard. 'Let's go', he says, draining the last of his pint. 'Your mother should be back on deck by now.' Standing, he folds the newspaper, and tucks it under his arm.

In the street, he drops the newspaper into the first rubbish bin we come across. As he does so, the cover sheet come adrift and we get one last look at the Page Three Girl.

———

Years later, on a trip from Hong Kong back to Australia, I visit my aunt. She's in her 90s, almost blind, but sharp as a tack. She offers me a beer and has one herself. Of seven children who made it to adulthood, she's the only one left. It must be a lonely space to occupy, but she doesn't complain. As usual, we grass-hop from one topic to another. She has an abiding interest in the state of the world, and rues the fact that her eyesight prevents her from Skyping grandchildren, nieces, and nephews.

As it often does, the conversation turns to my father. He was much older than she was, he being the second male sibling in the family and she the youngest female. He was fiercely protective of her in her teenage years, accompanying her to and from dances, vetting her suitors, that sort of thing.

'He stayed with us in Sydney on his way to visit you in England all those years ago', she says. 'One morning he sat on our front verandah polishing up his pair of brogues. He was so proud of those shoes—must have had them for about ten years.'

'At least,' I reply.

'"What are you up to, Bill?" I asked him.

'"I'm going to town to have lunch with Rupert", he said. Fancy that! He'd been retired for years, and Rupert still had time for him.'

I nod my head, not that she can see, and remain silent on the matter of Dad's Fallen Hero.

CATHOLIC DOGS

One day, when I was four, my mother decided it was time for me to go to school. There were two options in our suburb: Saint Mary's Catholic school or Burke Ward public school. My mother decided to send me to the Catholic school. I don't know whether this was because it was closer to home or because she was nominally a Catholic—I say 'nominally' because I never saw her in church. On the anniversary of her mother's death, she gave me money and a note for Father Leonard to say a mass to save Nan's soul. The Devil instructed me to throw the note away and use the money to buy cigarettes. For once I ignored him and dutifully presented the note and the money to the priest. I was pretty sure that Nan was capable of finding her way to heaven without the aid of Father Leonard, but I was too much of a coward to put this assumption to the test.

I had to walk to school like everyone else—everyone except the lucky kids who had a parent with a car and an inclination to drive them. We didn't have a car in those days. Our Dad had a bicycle which he rode to work. He carved a little wooden seat which he attached to the crossbar with a metal bracket, and occasionally, when the mood took him, would lift me on to it and take me for a ride.

Cousin Pete's dad, my Uncle Jimmy, had a car. It was a big beige Customline that he'd bought brand new. It was quite a rarity, that. Now and then he would drive us to school, but usually he just didn't have the inclination. He would drop Pete at our side gate, and we would walk to school. Slowly.

It was only two blocks to the Catholic school, but it seemed like forever and a day away. We would stop frequently to strip the bark from one of the gum trees that lined the street, throw rocks at things, or inspect a dead bird that had fallen off the overhead wiring. Our capacity for distraction was limitless. Shakespeare's schoolboy had nothing on us. The only kid slower was Johnny Dyer from down the street, but he was a cripple with leg irons and a crutch. Slow as we were, we'd often pass him as he struggled to school in the wake of his twin brother.

If we saw a gang of Protestant kids from the public school, we'd cross the street pretty smartly. They were a rough lot—the Atkins, the Bowens, and all the rest of them. Little Johnny never had a hope. They'd taunt him, call him 'Catholic dog', and sometimes push him over. I felt sorry for him; not that feeling sorry for someone got you anywhere in Broken Hill. Not in those days.

Later when we got bikes we would ride to school. But our progress wasn't much faster. We weren't supposed to ride on the footpath, but we always did. If the cops caught you, they'd box your ears and make you ride on the road where you became potential road kill.

One day the Protestant gang lay in wait for us. One of them shoved a broomstick handle in the front wheel of Pete's bike. The bike came to a dead stop, and Pete described a graceful parabola over the handlebars, landing on his face in the dirt. The bike cartwheeled after him and landed on his back. The Protestant kids laughed and ran away. That was the beginning of the War. In the beginning it was a phony War, as none of us was old enough to do real damage to each other; but all that would change, as you'll see.

Pete developed a knack for going arse-over-tit off his bike. One day, he was barrelling home from school along the footpath without looking where he was going and hit a sleeping dog. This had the same effect as the stick in the spokes trick. Pete somersaulted over the handlebars and hit the dirt. The bike came down on top of him. And then the dog jumped up and bit him on the leg. That time, he needed stitches in the head as well as his leg.

My first day at school didn't augur well for the future. Uncharacteristically, my mother had either forgotten or couldn't afford to buy me a school uniform, which consisted of grey flannel shorts and a blue shirt. She dressed me up in a yellow shirt and brown shorts. I turned up at school looking like an extremely junior member of the Hitler Youth—without the ribbons and badges. Even cousin Pete stayed away from me that day.

We were in kindergarten. We shared a large classroom with the first grade. There must have been well over a hundred kids in the class. The other classroom was occupied by the big kids—the second and third graders. Apart from a verandah, which was covered in wire mesh to prevent the Protestant kids from throwing bricks through the window, and a small office where the nuns hung out at lunch time, there was nothing much else to the school.

On that first day, Sister Mary Kosta announces that our major challenge for the year is to learn to read and write. I put up my hand. She ignores me for several minutes, and then turns on me.

'What is it?' she asks rather sharply. 'If you need to go to the toilet, you'll have to wait. You're in school now, and you have to learn discipline.'

'I can already read', I announce, somewhat smugly.

She stares at me. All I can see of her are her beady eyes, her beaky nose, and lipless mouth. The rest of the class are agog. After an eternity she thrusts a book at me.

'Show me', she says.

'This is Dick', I intone. 'This is Jane. This is Spot. See Spot run. Run, Spot, run.'

My fellow students gasp in awe.

'Tell your mother I want to see her tomorrow morning', snaps Sister Mary Kosta, and snatches the book away.

The next morning I wait outside the nuns' room while Sister Mary Kosta gives my mother a roasting. 'Why did you want to go and teach him to read?' she demands. 'What am I going to do with him now?'

'I didn't teach him to read', my mother protests on the verge of tears. 'He taught himself.'

My punishment for this act of independence was to spend the rest of the year, during reading lessons, sitting by myself at a table in the corner until the rest of the class catches up. That was fine by me. Now and then the other kids cast me envious looks. I would smirk back at them and, if Sister Mary Kosta wasn't looking, stick up my finger the way I'd seen the big kids do.

There were lots of diversions in the school yard. These often involved the police. One day, during morning recess, a big brown shaggy dog came tearing through the gate and began running around the yard in a demented way. It had a bloody wound in its throat, as though someone had tried to slit it. Sister Mary Margaret, who was on playground duty that day, tried to herd us into the classroom, but some of us hung out on the verandah behind the safety of the wire screen. The dog continued to run about yelping as though maddened by something. Eventually a police paddy wagon pulled up into the yard. Two police officers jumped out, cornered the dog, and shot it in the head. They then loaded the carcass into the back of the wagon and drove off. Ignoring the nuns, we rushed over to the spot where the dog had been shot and inspected the pool of blood that was drying in the gravel.

Usually, when a police car pulled into the school yard, it spelled bad news for someone. All the kids whose dads were on day shift would begin to tremble fearfully. The policeman would have a word to the sister in charge, who would then call one of the hapless kids out of the room. I can remember clearly the day that a police sergeant came to get Mollie Rickard. When the teacher called her out, she fainted dead away and had to be carried out to the police car. Later, we learned that her dad had been killed in a rock fall on the zinc mine. We envied Mollie because she got the rest of the week off school.

Next to the school was the Railwaytown Catholic church and the presbytery where Father Leonard, the local priest, lived. Father Leonard's nickname was 'Piggy' because that's what he looked like. He had the roundest, reddest face I've ever seen. Some years later, when I knew about these things, I learned that he was an alcoholic. In his younger days, the Church had been grooming him to be the next bishop of the parish, but he drank too heavily to be a bishop, which is hard to believe when you think about it. When he refused, or found it impossible, to give up his Cutty Sark, they packed him off to spend the rest of his days as a parish priest in Broken Hill, where he could blend in with his parishioners.

The church played a big part in our lives. My father was non-religious, but he never interfered with us. When it came to religion, he was supremely indifferent. Mother was what they called a lapsed Catholic, but she made us go to confession on Saturday afternoon and Mass on Sunday morning. We usually went to the earliest Mass, the one at seven o'clock in the morning, because you weren't allowed to touch food before taking Holy Communion. If you had anything to eat and then took Holy Communion, which was supposed to be the body of Christ, but which looked and tasted like a dry little wafer that glued itself to your tongue, you would go to Hell. Extremely devout parishioners refused even to swallow their saliva before sticking out their tongue and accepting the body of Christ. You took Communion at the altar rail, and then returned to you seat, with this wafer stuck to your tongue. You weren't even allowed to help it on its way with your finger. You just had to sit there while it slowly dissolved.

The other big no-no was to take Holy Communion in a state of mortal sin. Mortal sins ranged from murder through masturbation to eating meat on Friday. The Pope had the power to determine what was a mortal sin. One day, he decided that it was OK to eat meat on Friday. However, he died before adjudicating on masturbation, condemning every Catholic teenager (and presumably many adults as well) to make the Saturday afternoon trek to church for confession. Week in, week out, the formula remained the same.

'Bless me Father, for I have sinned. It's one week since my last confession. I had impure thoughts and touched myself.'

'Say three Hail Marys.'

Blessed and dismissed, I was free to receive Christ the following morning.

Once, in the heat of my teenage years, the Saturday afternoon ritual slipped my mind. I was out at the local abattoir riding the steers that were penned up waiting to be slaughtered the following Monday. I was there with Pete, my constant companion in those days, along with Lanky Richards and his pet dingo. (How things have changed. These days it's illegal to keep a dingo as a domestic pet.) Lanky's dad was the superintendent of the abattoir. If he caught us riding the steers, which he did occasionally, he'd beat the shit out of us. But Saturday afternoons were a pretty safe bet as he was invariably in the front bar of the Hillside Hotel with his cronies.

When I realised the time, I leapt in a panic from the steer to my bike.

'Where are you going?' asked Pete.

'Come on. We have to go to confession.'

'Oh, bugger that', he replied. His mother was much more relaxed about these things than mine.

When I got to the church, I was just in time to see Father Leonard's little car reversing out of the driveway of the presbytery. I hid behind the fence, knowing better than to get between Father Leonard and his afternoon whisky.

But now I was confronted with a dilemma. As I was in a state of mortal sin after a week of furious physical self-abuse, I would be unable to take communion the following day. And that would be noticed. I could skip mass, but that was also a mortal sin. I'd be piling sin upon sin, and my soul would be as black as night.

The following morning, I resolved the dilemma by slipping into church early and skulking in the choir loft with the other sinners.

If any of the Protestant kids caught you going in to church for Saturday confession or Sunday mass, they would set up a chant:

> *Catholic dogs*
> *Stink like frogs*
> *In a puddle of water!*

When I was eight, I became an altar boy. This necessitated learning Latin. We just learned it by rote and didn't have a clue what we were saying. The main reason for becoming an altar boy was that it got you out of school. However, becoming an altar boy was my undoing.

In order to be an altar boy, in addition to rote learning the Latin mass, I was required to wear a long, white smock. It had fancy lacing around the sleeves and neck and looked totally girly. Naturally, I took great care never to be seen outside the church in my altar boy's smock.

One Friday, it was my turn to prepare the church for benediction, which was like a kind of cut-down mass—mass lite, if you like. It was mercifully shorter than mass and didn't require the taking of Communion. One of the preparatory tasks was to heat a plug of charcoal over a spirit burner. This was dropped into a brass incense holder. The plug of charcoal caused the incense to smoulder, giving off a spicy aroma. During benediction, the priest waved the chalice around the church, filling it with sweet, sickly smoke. Most people liked the smell of incense; I thought that it smelled like death.

On this day, I go into the sacristy, light the spirit burner, and place the plug of charcoal in its holder. I remove the smock from its hook behind the door. As I'm pulling it over my head, the sleeve catches the spirit burner and pulls it over. I stare in horror as flames spread quickly over the wooden tabletop, and then I rush out of the church to find Father Leonard. Crossing the yard to the presbytery, I see a group of Protestant kids from the public school marching along the footpath under the supervision of a teacher. And they see me. Nothing is said, but Skinny Atkin looks me up and down and his lip curls, making his look like a mongrel dog.

At that moment Father Leonard emerges from the house. When I tell him of the calamity in the sacristy, he moves with remarkable speed for a fat little man, up the steps and into the sacristy. He snatches up a towel and beats out the flames. The table is ruined, but the rest of the sacristy is unharmed. He says nothing to me, but that was the last time I was given any independent responsibilities.

————

My mother is seriously ill, bedridden with double pneumonia. As a consequence, I'm staying at Pete's place. At the end of the school day, we wheel our bikes out of the schoolyard. Skinny and his mates are waiting across the street.

'There he is', says Skinny. 'Hey, you—Sheila, where's your dress?'

As we cycle home, Skinny and his mates follow us at a distance, predatory animals tracking their prey.

Pete and his family live on the edge of Railwaytown in the Old House, as we called it. This was the family home where my mother and her sisters grew up. Our family is considered slightly unusual because not only are Pete's mum and my mum sisters, our fathers are brothers. So the kids, all seven of us, come from identical genetic stock, and it shows.

The house, which was originally built in the 1890s, is set on several acres of ground. Like most houses in Broken Hill, it's constructed of corrugated iron. Over the years, various additions have been made and it's now a large, ramshackle place that has seen better days. It sits amid the ruins of what was once a magnificent garden. The garden was largely my mother's creation. She inherited a green thumb from somewhere or other and could bring what seemed to be dead twigs back to life, simply by a laying on of hands. When she married and moved away, the garden sank into decline.

Various outhouses punctuated the property. In addition to the mandatory outdoor lavatory, there was a ruined stable and the remains of what had been a zoo. My mother said that when she was a child, the zoo had contained kangaroos and wallabies, sulphur-crested cockatoos, galahs, an old wedge tailed eagle, a couple of goannas, and a one-eyed emu. The emu was bad-tempered and vicious and would chase you if you got on the side of its seeing eye.

The predators follow us all the way to the Old House. As we enter the front yard, they ride on by.

'Poofters!' calls out Skinny as he rides away. Pete sticks up his finger. I'm relieved that they've gone. Skinny was growing into a thorough brute. His father had done several spells in prison, and one of his older brothers was in reform school. Skinny was sure to go the same way.

We put our bikes in the shed and go into the house. Pete's mum is peeling potatoes. She gives us some orange cordial and yoyo biscuits. We take the biscuits out into the back yard and are standing near the corrugated iron fence, when *Whoomp!* A large lump of clay lands between us and disintegrates.

We leap apart. 'Shit!' says Pete, dropping his fizzy orange drink. He creeps to the fence and peeps over it, then immediately ducks down. 'Skinny and his mates', he whispers.

'Get out here, you little cunts', calls Skinny over the fence.

I'm shit scared, I have to confess. 'What'll we do?'

'I'm not scared', says Pete, but his quivering lower lip gives him away. Another lump of clay lands nearby. Peter runs through the back gate, and I follow him.

Out the back, between the fence and the low line of sand dunes, is a large claypan, the lumps of clay baked and cracked from the sun. Skinny and his mates are on the far side of the claypan. Pete, who has an amazing throwing arm and a deadly aim, picks up a lump of clay and pitches it straight at Skinny. Skinny ducks, laughs and pitches a lump straight back at Pete. Then it's on for young and old. The lumps of clay fly back and forth. Most miss their mark, although some come awfully close. All of a sudden I'm hit in the head with a lump that knocks me off clean off my feet. For a minute, I'm out cold. When I come to, I open my eyes. Pete is standing over me. Skinny and his mates have disappeared. Pete is holding half a house brick in his hand.

'Are you all right?'

'I dunno. I think so.'

I get to my feet and stagger around like a drunk.

'You don't look good.'

'I'm tired.'

Aunty Yon calls us to come and eat.

'What's for tea?' asks Pete.

'Sausages and mashed spuds.'

In the kitchen, I subside onto the couch. Every kitchen has a couch. It's where the neighbours sit to drink tea, where the kids languish when they're too sick to go to school.

Aunty Yon is listening to her favourite Elvis song.

It's one for the money, two for the show, three to get ready, now go, man go. But don't you step on my blue suede shoes!

'I don't want sobages', I say.

Aunty Yon looks at me. 'What's the matter with your voice?'

'He hit his head', says Pete.

Aunty Yon looks at the side of my head. There's a dent in my skull and a thin trickle of blood.

'You got quite a whack there', she says. 'But you'll be right. Good thing your Mum's sick in bed. She'd tick you off.' She gets me a clean tea towel and presses it to the side of my head. The wound doesn't bleed all that much, not like the other times I cut my head.

I go to sleep and wake to the smell of frying sausages. The smell makes me feel sick. I throw up all over the crocheted cover on the sofa.

'Don't worry, love', says my Aunt, and strips off the cover.

I doze again, wake up, throw up again. Pete and our brothers and sisters are eating sausages and mashed potatoes at the kitchen table.

Then something happens that saves my life. Uncle Don and Aunty Elva drop by. They're from the Protestant side of the family, but they're nice all the same. Aunty Elva is one of our Dad's many siblings.

'What's wrong with him?'

My eyes flutter open. Aunty Elva's perched on the edge of the couch.

'What happened to you?' She turns to my uncle. 'Don, we'd better get him to the hospital.'

Don is a massive tree of a man. I've always been slightly scared of him, not only because of his size but also because of his remoteness. Like a lot of men, he isn't quite sure how to act in the presence of children. However, he does exactly as his diminutive iron-willed wife says.

'He'll be all right. He got a whack on the head. Just a bit of concussion', says Aunty Yon. They take no notice of her, but bundle me in a blanket and carry me to the car.

Casualty at the Broken Hill and District Hospital is not a pleasant place to be on a Friday night. The waiting room is populated with footballers nursing dislocated shoulders and broken limbs, lacerated road accident victims, and drunks with a variety of self-inflicted injuries. Eventually, I'm inspected by one of the resident doctors and duly taken to the X-ray unit. One the X-rays have been completed, Aunty Elva says, 'Time to take you home'.

Instead of taking me back to the Old House, they take me to my real home. My father is elsewhere; probably at the

Musicians' Club, his usual Friday night haunt. My brother and sister are at the Old House. The only inhabitant of the house is my mother, propped up in one of the back bedrooms with double pneumonia. Dr Austin, our local physician, had tried to get her into hospital, but she refused. Aunty Elva shepherds me into the bedroom. My mother says nothing but gives me a reproachful look.

'I'm sorry', I say. I'm not sure why I say it. I'm the victim here, after all, but I say it anyway. And repeat it.

'Go to bed' is all she says. I find myself in the double marital bed, a towel protecting the pillow from my head. All I can hear is the low rumble of Uncle Don's voice from the bedroom down the hall. Drifting in and out of sleep, I bang my head against the pillow to try and clear the blocked sensation. I wake in the early hours to find my father looking at me from the doorway.

I sleep, wake, sleep, wake. Lose track of hours, days. It's evening. Dr Austin is standing at the foot of the bed along with my father, and, amazingly, my mother, who has dragged herself off her sickbed.

'I've been on to the phone to the brain surgeon in Adelaide', he says. 'By rights we should fly him there for the surgery, but there's a chance he wouldn't survive the trip. I asked Dr. Grey if he could come up and do the operation, but he can't get here tomorrow, and he says that time is essential. It has to be tomorrow. He has every confidence in me, which is reassuring. I've seen this surgical procedure before. The problem in this case is that the skull is compressed onto the brain, and so we can't use a spatula to lift it off without risking major damage. Death —or worse.'

'What could be worse than death?' asks my mother.

'Do you want to spend the rest of your life looking after a living vegetable?' he replies.

'If that's what we have to do', she says, and starts to cry.

At that, I start to bang my head on the pillow to clear the blocked feeling.

Instantly, Dr Austin is by my side, pinning my shoulders to the bed with his soft, plump hands.

'Don't do that, Laddie', he says. He always called me 'Laddie'. I guess he could never remember my name.

The children's ward at the Broken Hill and District Hospital is full, so they put me in the infants' ward. I wake up to find a nurse sitting by my side. She holds a steel basin containing a pair of scissors and a cut-throat razor. 'Time for a haircut', she says. A small child squats in the bed to my right. A lump of shit falls out of the leg of her nappy. She looks at it in surprise, as though it's a gift from heaven. And then picks it up and stuffs it into her mouth. Pretty soon her face is smeared in shit. The smell is revolting. The nurse laughs. 'Would you like a spoon, Sweetie?' she asks. The little kid gives her an angelic smile and gurgles. The nurse turns away and begins to shear my head.

I'm not allowed to get out of bed unaccompanied. When I need to go to the toilet, which is through the swing doors that define the ward, I have to push a call button and wait until someone comes to accompany me. Sometime they come. Sometimes they don't. I begin to wonder whether the shit-eating act on the part of the little girl in the bed next to me is a form of silent protest. Some time after my head has been shaved, I need to go. I push the button again and again. No-one comes. Eventually, I take myself to the toilet. I'm staring at myself in the mirror when the nurse and an orderly find me. Apart from the huge dent to the right side of my cranium, my head is as smooth and domed like a large egg. The nurse starts shouting at me. The orderly grabs me in an ungainly bear hug and bundles me back into bed.

Dawn is just beginning to break when the lights in the ward are switched on. The big clock over the door tells me it's six o'clock. Some of the babies wake and begin to cry. The others slumber on. A nurse dumps an olive green overall on my bed. 'Here's your giggle suit', she says. 'Put it on.' She's different from the one who shaved my head and shouted at me last night. Her voice sounds strange. Later, I learn that she's German.

The nurses might have changed, but the orderly remains the same—a bald man with a big nose. This morning he too is dressed in a pair of olive-coloured overalls. He picks me up as though I weigh nothing and deposits me onto a trolley, then pushes me through the swinging doors of the ward.

You get a very different view of the world when you're flat on your back and propelled through corridors, into elevators, and into an operating theatre. Faces loom over you. People are wearing olive-green skull caps and masks. Without knowing why, you begin to say Hail Marys over and over again.

Hail Mary full of grace the Lord is with Thee. Blessed art Thou among men and blessed is the fruit of Thy womb, Jesus. Holy Mary, Mother of God, pray for us sinner, now and at the hour of our death. Amen.

Is that it? Is this to be my last few minutes?

My thoughts are interrupted by a large soft face. Strands of sandy hair stray out from under his skull cap. 'Hello Laddie', the mouth says. Another face appears. 'I'm just going to pop this mask over your face', it says. 'I want you to breathe deeply and count to ten.'

Then a horrible thing happens. A rubber cone is jammed onto my face, and I'm being suffocated. My lungs fill with some putrid, poisonous gas. They have brought me here not to save me, but to kill me. I try to tear the mask off my face, but someone has my arms pinned down. Desperately, I shake my head from side to side. And then I spin off into infinity.

I wake up back in the ward vomiting foul black bile into a silver kidney dish. A nurse notices that I'm awake and glides across the ward. She perches on the edge of the bed and support my head as I vomit again. The smell is disgusting, but then hospitals are full of vile smells.

I have a raging thirst. I ask for water, but my request comes out as a barely coherent croak. The nurse seems to know what I want. She gives me some chips of ice from a metal container beside the bed. 'You can't have water yet', she says. 'You'll only throw it up. And that won't be any good, will it?' I don't care. I'm desperate for water. The ice chips do nothing for me. My head flops back onto the pillow and I sink back into sleep.

And that is how most of the day passes, drifting between semi-consciousness and sleep, coming to periodically to vomit into the kidney bowl.

Midway through the afternoon a slight commotion wakes me up. The clock suspended over the swing doors tells me it's 3.30. Nursing aides push trolleys into the ward and begin washing and changing the children and generally tidying up the place. One of them points to me and asks the charge sister if I should get the treatment as well. The charge sister shakes her head. 'He won't be getting any visitors', she says.

And she's right. At four o'clock, the swing doors are propped open and visitors stream in. Parents and grandparents coo at their children. The older ones receive chocolate bars, colouring-in books and other small gifts. The only patients who receive no visitors are me and the little shit-eating kid in the bed to my right. She hauls herself up by the bars that keep her penned in the bed and begins to cry. I notice that one of her legs is shorter than the other. There is also something strange about her eyes. They make her look slightly mongoloid. Maybe she *is* slightly mongoloid. That could be the reason no-one has come to visit her.

I knew my mother couldn't come, that she was bedridden herself, and that my father wouldn't come because he had a newspaper to print. But I did think that someone would could—a spare aunty or cousin. But no-one. Those two visiting hours seemed interminable. I was glad when visiting time was over and the visitors were ushered out of the room, even though it meant that the smaller kids began to cry.

As soon as the last of the visitors have straggled out of the room, the orderlies serve tea. I'm disgusted by the smell and want to throw up again, but my throat is raw and my stomach is empty. The orderly offers me a tray, but I turn away, so she shrugs and leaves the tray on the metal locker beside my bed. The small children have to be fed by hand, which keeps the orderlies pretty occupied. They're not in the slightest bit interested into trying to coax me in to eating.

I doze off, and then at seven p.m. wake to see my father poking his head through the door. He spots me and comes towards me with one of those fake, cheery grins that people wear when visiting the sick. He perches on the edge of the bed, and I can smell the beer on his breath.

'How are you son?' he asks.

How am I? Dying, perhaps. 'All right', I reply, in a small voice.

'Got a bit of a turban on, eh? They've turned you into an Indian.'

I reach up and pat the bandage swathing my head. I have no idea what a turban is, but guess that's what he's talking about. He fishes in his pocket and pulls out a Cadbury's fruit-and-nut chocolate bar.

'Got you this', he says, and puts it on the locker. After that, the conversation pretty well fizzles out. He sits there a little while longer, inspecting the other children in the ward, and then says, 'Well, I'd better go see how your mother is getting on.'

'All right', I say, and close my eyes. Later in the evening, I wake and decide to have some of the chocolate bar, but it is gone.

As it happens, Dr Austin lives three doors down the street from us in a large brick house. It's the only house in the street that isn't built of corrugated iron. He lives there with his wife, who is also a physician, and two colourless little children. It's very convenient having the local doctor just down the street. When we break bones, inflict wounds on each other with hunting knives, burn ourselves, or step on broken glass, we're rushed along the street, where Dr Austin attends to us in the front room that he uses as a surgery.

The morning after the operation, Dr Austin does his rounds accompanied by the hospital matron and a nurse.

The matron's name is Sister Ralph. She's the mother of Trevor, one of my classmates. Apparently, it's a big deal for her to make a personal visit.

Dr Austin gives me one of his watery smiles.

'How are we, Laddie?' he asks.

I have no idea how he is, but I say, 'All right.'

'You're a very lucky young man.'

'I know', I say.

'You do?'

'I woke up', I say. 'During the operation.'

Matron Ralph looks startled. The nurse snorts out loud. Dr Austin gives me an indulgent look. 'That's impossible, Laddie, you had anaesthetic. You were asleep during the whole operation.'

'I woke up when you drilled into my head.'

When I say this, Dr Austin looks at Matron Ralph. There was no way I could have known that he'd saved my life by drilling into my skull. Only later does my mother tell that the surgery was touch and go, that when he'd removed my scalp, he found that the skull was so deeply compressed onto the brain that he was unable to insert a spatula to raise the bone. He'd called the brain specialist in Adelaide, who had talked him through the procedure of drilling into the skull, inserting screws, and lifting the skull off the brain.

Upset at their scepticism, I do what all kids do to get themselves out of a tight spot. I lie.

'I saw Jesus', I say. Matron Ralph is a devout Catholic. My friend Trevor and his big brother Dennis are Catholic dogs. She has to believe me.

It doesn't wash with Dr Austin, who is a Protestant. He signals to the nurse, who removes my turban so that he can admire his handiwork, and then nods to the nurse who swabs the wound and replaces the bloody turban with a clean one.

Later that afternoon, my Aunty Yon comes to see me. More cheery, cheesy grins. She too asks me how I am. She also gives me a Cadbury's chocolate bar. She tells me that the whole school went to the church and prayed for my soul while I was being operated on. I guess there are times when it pays to be a Catholic dog. After she has left, I close my eyes. Presently, sensing movement by the bed, I open them again. The nurse with the strange accent is slipping the chocolate bar into the pocket of her uniform.

I have been given strict instructions not to get out of bed unaided. I'm not even supposed to stand up without assistance. For several days I do as I'm told, but then the crippling boredom of being confined to bed becomes too much.

The walls separating the wards do not go all the way to the ceiling. One day, curious as to what's going on in the adjoining ward, I climb onto the metal locker and peer over the wall into the next ward. This is the ward that I should be in. It's occupied by kids about my age, not with shit-eating babies. One of them sees me hanging over the top of the wall like a little albino Indian in my turban and calls out to the other kids in the ward. I laugh and give them the finger. Pretty soon there's a right old commotion going on.

The duty nurse rushes into the ward and sees me hanging over the wall. Before I know it, I'm being hauled off the wall. One of the orderlies holds me down while the other goes to the nursing station. When he returns, he is carrying a strange looking jacket. It opens down the back and has extremely long sleeves. I later learn that it's called a straitjacket. The orderlies force me into the jacket, crossing my arms across my chest and passing the ends of the strait-jacket behind my back. They tie the ends to the bed rails. I am a prisoner on the bed, trussed up like a chicken, immobilised on my back. I try to bite the hand of the orderly, but he grins and walks away. I call out, but no one comes. The little shit-eating mongoloid kid in the next bed looks at me curiously.

After what seems like hours, but, according to the clock on the wall is only twenty-five minutes, Matron Ralph happens into the ward. When she seems me all trussed up, an angry flush crosses her face. She turns, marches out through the swinging doors, and returns a few seconds later with the duty nurse.

'What's all this?' she demands.

'He was out of bed', replies the foreign-sounding duty nurse—the evil one who stole my chocolates.

Matron and the nurse disappear. A minute later, one of the orderlies appears and sets me free. Immediately, I turn my face to the wall and, filled with self-pity, silently cry.

———

Dr Austin is pleased with my progress. It's been three weeks. He decides that I can go home. He sits on the edge of the bed and gives me a lecture on what not to do. The list is quite long and includes no physical activities. No football. No boxing. No fighting. Especially no fighting.

———

It's 1971 and the Vietnam War rages on. The government had run short of young men to send to Saigon to be killed, so they institute a draft system. Not all young men are required to serve, however, just those whose birthdays are plucked out of a ballot. In the fullness of time, my number comes up. I'm not averse to serving my country—although, like millions of other Australians, I'm opposed to the Vietnam War, and I'm incensed at the injustice of the ballot. If one has to go, all should have to serve. I receive an official letter telling me where and when I should present myself for my medical. I'm instructed to bring along any relevant medical records.

I manage to track down Dr Austin, who has a practice on the outskirts of Sydney. I call him up, remind him of my existence, and request a letter detailing my life-threatening head injury years ago in Broken Hill.

'Why? Aren't you prepared to serve your country like decent young people?' he asks. Without waiting for an answer, he says, 'You'll get no letter from me', and hangs up the phone.

Whatever happened to the injunction not to fight? I wonder.

ROAD KILL

There was a lot of it about in those days—death, that is. Hardly surprising in a mining town squatting in the middle of nowhere, enduring the hard light and hostility of the Australian bush. A town that the rest of the country cared little about, and that the rest of the world cared nothing about—if, indeed, it had heard about Broken Hill. Although it was in the middle of nowhere, it wasn't in the geographical centre of no-where. That distinction belonged to Alice Springs, or 'The Alice'. So even in terms of location, it couldn't quite get it right.

Even today, white people cling to the coast. Spend time alone under the stars out there in the middle of nowhere and you'll soon find out you're not wanted. Try it some time. You'll see what I mean. In my younger days, I spent many nights camping under the stars, feeling the presence of an alien, almost malevolent spirit moving through the scrub, throbbing in the night air.

In Broken Hill, death came in various shapes and forms. On the mines, it usually came suddenly and violently, as a stope collapsed. Or a shower of rocks rained down on a working party. Or a miner, careless for a second, stepped backwards down an uncovered shaft. As kids, we got used to the police car in the schoolyard, the sobbing kid being driven away, the inevitable funeral that left from the church beside the school. It seemed to happen every other week, but that's probably just my imagination working overtime.

And then there was suicide. Our town was the suicide capital of the country. Guns were everywhere: under beds, in the boots of cars, sitting in racks in the shed at the bottom of the yard. Everybody had at least one. When we turned twelve we were allowed BB guns, or 'slug guns' as we called them. At fifteen we graduated to .22 rifles, then later on, to .303s. All strictly illegal, of course, but then this was Broken Hill, and Broken Hill made its own laws.

Shotguns were for men, although I never cared for them. When I was twelve, my Uncle Jack took me up the river and let me shoot at a flight of ducks. The ducks couldn't have been safer, but because I didn't pull the stock tightly into my shoulder as I'd been instructed to do, the recoil knocked me clean off my feet. I was knocked unconscious and concussed for several days.

In my later teens I had a handgun, a police issue Webley 38. I bought it from the Belgian codger Willie, who was said to have been a mercenary in the Congo. How he ended up in Broken Hill I never knew. And didn't care. There were lots of people without a past in Broken Hill.

When it came to suicide, some people chose to go out in style, like my dad's mate Fred, who helped himself to a stick of gelignite from the mine and blew himself to smithereens in the Thackaringa Hills. There some debate in the pub as to whether Fred had really meant to top himself or whether it had been an accident. The consensus, however, was that Fred was too good with explosives for it to be an accident. There certainly wasn't much of him left for the undertaker to work with.

Some opted for the rope. But with guns everywhere, most took the easy way out. Like Maureen Roberts' dad. The Roberts' house was in the lane behind ours. Maureen was a girl of unapproachable beauty. In junior high school, I had a desperate crush on her, but never dared speak to her. It happened late at night, as it usually did. I was woken by the sharp report of a .22, followed by silence. Then all hell broke loose: footfalls up and down the street; a young girl screaming uncontrollably. In school, the following day, Maureen's cousin told us that she'd walked in on him at the very instant that he'd pulled the trigger.

The other lethal weapon was the car. When it came to death, cars gave you a wide range of options, both intended and otherwise. Those intent on ending it all but who had no taste for the cold end of a rifle barrel could stick one end of a hosepipe into the exhaust pipe and the other end into the car. Switch on the ignition and let the car idle for a few minutes, and you would slip into a deep, permanent sleep. Another option, and one favoured by those who wanted their demise to look like an accident rather than suicide, was to get up to speed on the Barrier Highway and drive headlong into an oncoming road train. That method was messy, selfish, and not always guaranteed to succeed.

The vast majority of road deaths were not by design but the result of alcohol, poorly engineered roads, and a combination of teenage bravado and inexperience. Drag races pushed cars way beyond their limits, and many of them simply fell apart. When that happens at 100 miles an hour, the result is spectacular—and almost inevitably fatal.

A rite of passage for any young man with a newly acquired car was to 'crack the ton', which meant pushing the car to exceed 100 miles an hour. In a newly acquired car, this was unwise. As the car, commonly called a 'jalopy', was invariably third-, fourth-, or even fifth-hand, it was downright foolhardy. Many of these cars were only capable of exceeding 100 miles an hour if they were pushed beyond their limit on a downhill run.

The rite of passage worked like this. Having scraped and saved for months, a Saturday morning arrives when a mate, who has already acquired his car, picks you up and drives you across town to meet a bloke he knows who has a car for sale. It's a good buy, he assures you. You are doubtful at first. Wouldn't it be better to go to a reputable second-hand car dealer who would offer a warranty? The mate scoffs. With sales tax and the dealer's cut, the car would cost you twice as much. So you agree to look at the car, a 1957 FJ Holden, an Australian icon. Suddenly you're excited. This car could actually be yours! Sure, the Duco has worn through in patches, and bits of stuffing are escaping from the split in the driver's seat. But Barry the welder down the street could reattach the front bumper in no time.

Ownership papers and money change hands. You'll deal with the registration next week. Crunching the gears, you drive it home, detouring down Argent Street in the hope that some of your mates—or better still, one of the girls you've had your eye on—will notice you. (They don't!) Back home, you wash the car and polish it up as best you can. Your Old Man, home from the pub, gives the car a sideways glance and mutters something as he passes. Did he say 'Waste of fucking money!'?

Late afternoon, you do several slow laps of Argent Street. Finally, little Mickey notices you and jumps into the passenger's seat. You manage to find a parking space in front of the Orange Spot slap bang in the middle of town where no one can possibly miss you. You and Mickey join your other mates in the back bar of the Royal Exchange. Beer flows, and so too does good-natured ribbing. When 'last orders' is called, Jeff 'Barney' Rubble turns to you and says, 'So, show us what she'll do.' The rite of passage begins.

There are seven of you: four in the back, you and two others in the front. With a can of beer in hand, you head out on the Menindee Road, figuring that the steep descent from the crest of the Thackaringa Loop is your best way of cajoling the aging FJ over the ton. You cross the railway track that runs 700 hundred miles east to Sydney, and get the feel of the car on the open road as you ease it on to the slow right hand curve that takes you out towards Sydney. There are butterflies in your stomach, but your fear is dulled by the alcohol. You flatten your foot. The car responds sluggishly. More ribaldry. 'What's up, mate? Can't you find the pedal?' Laughter. The night is clear. The moon throws a cold light on the spinifex and saltbush that stretch away from the side of the road. You get the car up to 70 on the straight, which is a good omen, but are nearly undone when, on approaching the Thackaringa Range, a giant Big Red kangaroo—he must be eight feet tall at least—appears in the headlight from nowhere and bounds across the road. You miss him by inches.

You crest the ridge. The canopy of stars hangs low, from here to infinity. Far below you see the lights of the Rockwell

Pub. 'Gun it!' Barney calls from the back seat, and you do. Whoops from the alcohol fuelled troops. The engine screams, but gravity does most of the work. Halfway down the long incline, the front bumper bar is ripped away and sails off into the darkness. Little Mickey keeps his eye on the speedometer. 'Seventy-five!' he shouts. 'Eighty!' 'Get your arse in gear', calls someone from the back. 'Ninety! Ninety-five!'

You are approaching the bottom of the hill now. Your foot is pressed to the floor. 'Ninety-eight', shouts Mickey. 'Nearly there.' As he speaks, the car hits the spoon-drain at the bottom of the hill with an enormous bang and is airborne. 'A hundred and five!' calls Mickey in triumph. You have passed your Rite of Passage. Cheers from in the back, although you can feel the fear. The car is airborne for an age, and while it's in the air you have no control. You swing the steering wheel from side to side, although common sense should have told you to keep the wheels straight.

When the car makes contact with the road again, the front wheels are angled at sixty degrees to the road. The car immediately flips, and flips, and flips again, cartwheeling down the road at horrific speed, crushed until it's barely recognizable. Inside, bodies are flung helplessly about. A rear door flies open and two of the inhabitants are shot out onto the road. The car continues to flip. 'Please make it stop', you pray. Eventually it does, resting on its roof. Silence apart from the tinkle of glass falling onto the asphalt, the steady drip of petrol, and the sound of spinning wheels that just won't stop. You haul yourself through the driver's side window, cutting your hand as you do so, and crawl to the side of the road. Only little Mickey is upright, wandering aimlessly in circles, saying something that doesn't make sense. Behind the wreck, the road is littered with motionless bodies. The last thing you remember is the sound of running feet coming from the pub.

Our house, like 90 percent of the houses in Broken Hill, was clad with corrugated iron. This was good and bad. It was good because corrugated iron houses were cheap and easy to construct. It was bad because in winter it was as cold inside as it was out. 'As cold as charity', the neighbours would say to one another, rubbing their hands. In summer, the scorching sun sucked all of the oxygen out of the air, and it was hotter indoors then it was out. On many nights, we were driven outside to sleep on canvas stretchers in the backyard where the mosquitoes ate us alive. But at least we could breathe.

Our little corner of Broken Hill was quiet; sleepier even than most of the town because it was enfolded by a ridge of hills. Our house sat at the intersection of Cornish and Nichol Streets. It faced Cornish Street, a bituminised strip that ran up over Cornish Street Hill. The intersecting street, Nichol Street, more or less fizzled out when it collided with Cornish Street, becoming a harmless dirt strip meandering up the right-hand side of our house. It ended in a cul-de-sac at the bottom of a steep hill that overlooked the entire western end of the town. The hill was punctuated with rocky outcrops and covered with saltbush and tumbleweeds that blew down into our yard. Several houses had been built on the crest of the hill, but apart from these, the hillside was inhabited only by a flock of tethered goats and little waxbill finches that flitted amongst the saltbush. The houses on the ridge could only be accessed from the other side, where the gradient was gentler. We used to roam the hillside playing bandits, lighting fires, throwing stones at the tethered goats, and terrorizing the pensioners who lived at the top of the hill.

———

One day when I was six or seven, this sleepy corner of town was disrupted by the abrupt arrival of heavy earth-moving equipment, large yellow monsters that groaned and crashed and shook the foundations of our house as they were unloaded from the jinkers that transported them. When they roared into life, the noise and the stench of diesel drove our normally placid mother crazy.

'What's going on?' she demanded of my father when he came home from work.

'What's going on? I'll tell you what's going on. They're building a road over the bloody hill, that's what's going on.'

Apparently, one night after several drinks too many too many, the Chief Engineer of the Barrier District Council had bet the Assistant Engineer that he couldn't put a road over the nearly vertical hillside. The Assistant Engineer, who had also had a drink too many, accepted the wager, and so the work began.

The adults in the neighbourhood were appalled. At the end of each working day, the heavy equipment would be lined up along our side fence like the tanks and trucks of an invading army. My mother would then take a bucket of warm soapy water and scrub the accumulated cracker dust from of the kitchen walls, muttering under her breath as her perspiration mingled with the dirty soap suds in the bucket.

We kids loved it. We would sit in the dirt marvelling at the bulldozers as they reared on their ends in an effort to breach the hill. The last few yards below the crest, which was the steepest part of the hill, had to be finished by hand. I can remember the immigrant workers swearing, slipping and sliding in the dust as they struggled to win the wager for the Assistant City Engineer.

One day the Atkin boys from down the street appeared at the top of the hill and began pelting the workers with rocks. The workers dropped their picks as shovels and ran after the Atkin boys, cursing and waving their fists. But they never stood a chance. Even Skinny, the middle brother (called 'Skinny' because he carried an extra load of fat around his waist), had no trouble evading the workers. Like a band of brigands or insurgents, they simply melted into the hillside. The workers were forced to abandon the chase and return to the challenge of finishing their impossible road.

A little while later, the Atkins appear from a side lane at the bottom of the hill. Skinny sees me, comes over and sits next to me in the gutter. We weren't supposed to talk to the Atkins. Mother thought they were 'common' because their father was in prison and their mother had no front teeth. I never knew what my Father thought. He usually kept his opinions about other people to himself. The Atkins had the rest of the neighbourhood kids, and some of the adults, intimidated. Mickey had just come home from reform school. Skinny was on probation. Peter, like his mother, was missing a front tooth.

The Atkins usually ignored me. I was small beer—not

significant enough to notice. But on this day there is no-one else on offer. They shout abuse at the workers struggling away at the top of the hill. The workers, however, ignore them.

The baker with his horse and cart clip-clops past along the cross street. I liked the baker. He was a kind man who sometimes let me ride with him. He'd give me a loaf of bread that had fallen on the road, and I would pull out the warm, doughy centre. The smell of warm bread, horse shit, and sweaty hide was curiously alluring. Occasionally, when the horse let go of a dump outside our house, Mum would hurry out with a bucket and shovel, scoop it up, and spread it on the garden.

As the baker passes, Skinny throws a rock to make the horse bolt. It misses the horse, but clatters off the cart. The baker sticks his head out to see who hurled the rock. When he sees me with the Atkins, he gives me a disappointed look.

Mickey Atkin, the senior member of the gang of brothers and the leader of the pack, looks at me. Then he picks up a pot of tar that the workmen have left with a collection of other tools at the bottom of the hill. Their tools were constantly being pilfered, but the workers didn't seem to mind. He looks at his brothers and laughs. Skinny pushes me over into the dirt and sits on my chest. Peter, the youngest—who, in fact, is only a couple of years older than me—sits on my legs. Mickey dips the brush into the tar pot and paints my face. I keep my eyes and mouth closed tight, but the tar still gets in. It's hot, and it burns my skin.

When he has finished, Mickey says to his youngest brother. 'Peter, we need feathers. Go and get some feathers.'

Peter gets up off my legs. He looks around. He's a bit

simple, Peter; not that his brothers are all that bright. 'Where... where... what feathers?'

'Use your fuckin' brains—if you got any', says Skinny. 'The Heslops have chooks.'

The Heslops live up the lane; their house adjoins the Atkins' ramshackle dump. Peter runs off to find feathers. While he is gone, I start to cry. Skinny tells me to shut up, but Mickey just laughs. After a while, Peter comes back with a handful of feathers.

I don't remember my mother saying a word. She heats water and starts the slow process of removing the tar and feathers from my face. As she removes the tar, half of my face comes with it. As she picks the tar from my face, her hand wrapped in a hot towel, silent tears run down her cheeks. I feel sorry for her, although not as sorry as I feel for myself. It is the first time I remember seeing her cry. When she has removed as much of the tar as she can, she puts me to bed and walks down the street to speak to Mrs Atkin.

———

Eventually, the road was finished. Initially they tried to bituminise it, but realised that it was too steep and soon gave up. So it remained a limestone scar running down the face of what was virtually a cliff. Cars brave enough to inch their way down the hill left a pall of white dust hanging in the air. The dust eventually invaded the interstices of the surrounding houses, leaving a fine film on anything that didn't move.

My cousins and I constructed a billy cart from a vegetable crate, a fence paling, and the wheels off an old pram. It took three of us to get to the top of the hill, hauling the cart up the meandering side track that ran beside the road. Along the way, we collected a motley band of neighbourhood waifs, all anxious to share vicariously in this initial assault on the road.

On the crest of the hill, we were presented with the terrifying reality of the road. Basically it disappeared beneath our feet. You might as well have been standing on the edge of a precipice. We argued among ourselves over who was to have the honour of test-driving the billy car. Finally, my older cousin Robert, who was the brains of our little band and had masterminded this escapade, turned on the bunch of neighbourhood kids and pointed to Paddy Flynn, a snot-nosed little kid with an Irish accent.

'Get in', he said.

Paddy showed a distinct disinclination to accept this honour. We had to drag him to the cart, make him take a firm grip on the length of cord that was meant to steer the car, and shove him off into space. He took off immediately at terrifying speed. Things seemed to be going well until the cart disintegrated halfway down the hill. Paddy made a spectacular arc in the air and then slid down the rest of the hill like a baseball player trying to make it to first base. His big brother scrambled down the hill after him. Paddy was covered in cuts and his clothes were ripped to shreds, but nothing appeared to be broken. His brother pulled him upright and tried to dust him down. 'Don't tell Mam', he said in his Irish brogue as he led his little brother away. We vacated the hill as well, abandoning the wrecked billy cart by the side of the road. 'Don't tell Mum.' For years, that was our mantra when anything went wrong.

———

Accidents involving cars were rare at first but occurred with increasing frequency as word spread around town about the thrill of the hill. The problem was that most cars found it impossible to pull up before encountering the Cornish Street intersection. It was only a matter of time before the inevitable occurred. Early one evening, as we were sitting down to have our evening meal—'tea' as it was called—there was a terrific crash.

We all rush on to the front verandah. Two cars have collided with terrific force, rolling one of them onto its side. It lies like a wounded animal, its wheels spinning uselessly in the air and petrol leaking into the gutter. The driver tries unsuccessfully to climb out through the side window. The driver of the car that is still upright has put his face through the windscreen of the car. He gets out of the car, lurches across the road, and sits with his back against our front fence.

'Get inside, you kids', says Mum. We ignore her, fascinated by the drama that is being played out on the street. Mum rushes inside to call an ambulance.

Neighbours come from all directions. Several of them push the overturned car upright and help the driver out. He collapses onto the road, although he doesn't seem as badly injured as the other driver. He isn't bleeding at all, which I find slightly disappointing.

After the first one, accidents became more frequent. The peak time for accidents was on weekends. Most accident victims favoured late Saturday night, with a minority preference for Sunday afternoon. The trick was to gun your car over the hill from the gentler side and get all four wheels to leave the ground. It must have been such a rush. I will never forget the first time I rode my bike over the hill. You couldn't see the road ahead. It was just like launching yourself over a cliff. I never got to go over the hill in a car, but it must have been a lot of fun, especially on a Saturday night.

Nichols Street Hill became a local tourist feature. Kids gravitated from all over town to challenge it on bikes or in billy carts. Getting down with rider and equipment intact was a major challenge. It was a bit like conquering Mt. Everest in reverse. Within weeks, every motorist in town had tested their car and their nerve on the hill, although the vast majority did it as sedately as possible, creeping over the crest of the hill and gently riding the brake to the bottom. Too heavy a foot on the brake, and the car was likely to go into a slide on the gravel and roll over. I saw that happen more than once.

Our lives didn't change for the better with the breaching of the hill. The furniture was covered with a permanent film of dust, which bothered our mother much more than it bothered us. It was the cars that bothered us. When Nichols Street had ended in a cul-de-sac, it was a public space, almost like a neighbourhood park where housewives met to gossip and kids played marbles and bully-on-a-string. Now you crossed the street at your peril.

But most intrusive was the noise. In winter, huddled under the blankets, pillow wrapped around our heads, we'd be roused from sleep in the small hours of Sunday morning as cars roared over the hill, one after the other, like an invading army. The rattle and roar was followed by a scream of brakes as drivers attempted to stop their cars before hitting the intersection. Now and then there would be a tremendous explosion when one car collided with another, or the driver lost control and ploughed into the sturdy euca-lypt that stood sentinel at the intersection of Cornish and Nichols Street—incidentally turning the intersection into a blind cornet for anyone coming down the hill or driving west on Cornish Street.

At first, whenever an accident occurred, we would leap out of bed and rush onto the verandah, but soon we grew blasé and barely stirred from sleep. The accidents them-selves varied from relatively minor to life threatening; although, miraculously, in the first few months there were no fatalities. An accident involving only minor injuries and damage was usually followed by a great deal of cursing and reciprocal abuse as the alcohol-fuelled drivers and their passengers examined the damage to their cars and blamed each other for the accident. This would go on until a neigh-bour appeared at his window and told them to shut up.

Occasionally a fight would break out. Then police and tow trucks would arrive, and there would be even more noise before the night became silent and dark once more. When someone was injured, it usually spelled the end of our peace for the night. Ambulances and paramedics would arrive along with the police. The police parked their vehi-cles with lights on high beam, illuminating the accident scene as well as our house. Once the seriously injured had been dispatched to the hospital, the police interviewed those who had survived relatively unscathed. They also, mysteriously, took elaborate measurements and made marks on the road. I asked my Dad why they did this. He shrugged, and said, not very helpfully, 'It's what they do—police work.' Dad had veiled contempt for anyone occupa-tion that did not involve printing newspapers. If the accident had been a bad one involving multiple victims, in the morning we would venture out and look at the bloodstains on the road.

Sundays followed a familiar pattern. If I got up in time, I went to seven o'clock mass. That way I could receive the Body of Christ before starving to death. Even half a dry crust eaten before Mass was enough to disqualify you from receiving the Body of Christ, which was kind of ironic, because that's the form he came in—Christ, a dry tablet of unleavened bread that adhered instantly to the room of the mouth and had to be prised off with the tongue. Only the priest was allowed to lay hands on the Body of Christ.

The rest of the morning was spent either raiding the fruit trees of the pensioners in the neighbourhood or hanging around at home in a state of listless stupefaction. At around noon our Dad went to the Musicians' Club while Mum tried to prevent the Sunday roast from becoming hopelessly overcooked. We kids attempted to stave off death from starvation by sneaking into the kitchen when Mum wasn't looking and stealing slices of bread and jam. Finally, at around 2 p.m. a car would pull up at the side gate, and one of Dad's brothers, usually Jimmy, would drop him off.

We'd rush to the kitchen, bolt down our food, and then were forced to sit at the table until Dad gave us permission to leave. He would consume his lunch slowly, his head bowed over his plate as though eating were some kind of punishment. Mum would stand at the sink scraping scraps from our plates into a plastic bucket. These would later be hurled into the chicken pen at the bottom of the yard.

There were strict rules the governed the taking of food in our house, like 'Don't put your elbows on the table!' Like

'Eat your vegetables before your meat!' Like 'Always leave the table feeling you could eat some more!' Like 'Don't leave the table until everyone else has finished!'

When we were smaller there was another rule: 'Don't speak unless you're spoken to.' That rule went by the board a few years ago, although 'Don't speak while adults are talking' was still in force.

———

The car comes over the hill just as Dad is putting down his knife and fork, signalling that he has had his fill and that we are free to leave. There's a sound of rubber on gravel as the driver makes the mistake of trying to brake. He over-corrects, loses control, and we listen, frozen at the table, as the car rolls over and over before slamming into our side fence. It's a new fence. Dad and his brothers, Jimmy and Jack, spent several Sunday mornings erecting it not a month ago.

'Jesus!' says Dad, getting to his feet. He hardly ever swears, so we know that this is serious. We rush out of the house in his wake and see a late-model Ford resting on its side against our new back fence. Except that it's not quite so new any more.

Rather than wooden uprights, which eventually get eaten out by termites, Dad and his brothers used lengths of steel water pipe that had mysteriously appeared one night by the shed at the back of the house.

The uprights are steadfast and haven't moved, but the corrugated iron sheets are mangled. Wooden uprights would have snapped, and the car would probably have ended up in the kitchen with us.

On its wild ride down the hill, there were four people in the car. Three of them have struggled out of the upturned car and are wandering around in a daze. Two of them are bleeding. A third looks at his left arm, which is dangling uselessly at his side. The fourth person had been thrown out of the car as it rolled over. He is lying on his back in the gravel at the edge of the road; his eyes are closed and he is very still.

Dad turns briefly, and says 'You kids, get back inside the house!' Horrified and thrilled at this catastrophe, we scuttle around the back shed and climb into the cedar tree at the bottom of the yard. Here, screened by a canopy of leaves, we can watch unseen as the Sunday afternoon drama unfolds.

One of the men, who is bleeding from the forehead, says something to Dad. Holding a bit of rag to his head, the man removes rifles and a couple of shotguns from the back of the car and hands them over the fence to Dad, who puts them on the ground and covers them with a tarpaulin from the shed. He also passes Dad bottles of beer, which mysteriously survived the accident. Dad puts these in the shed.

I wonder why they need to hide the guns and beer. Later, Mum says you're not supposed to drive around town on a Sunday afternoon with such things. I could never figure out the rules of the town. They seemed so arbitrary. I guess that's why I eventually left.

The police paddy wagon arrives shortly before the ambulance. By this time, most of the neighbours are clustered around the figure on the side of the road. Two policemen with big stomachs get out of the wagon and push their way through the crowd. One scratches his head. The other one nods to Dad. They're drinking mates at the Musicians' Club. Then he gets down on one knee beside the accident victim.

Curiosity gets the better of me. I slip down the tree and creep over to take a closer look before Dad herds me back behind the fence. The body belongs to Mickey Atkin. He looks quite small, and not at all scary, lying there. Apart from a bloody graze on his forehead, there doesn't seem to be anything wrong with him. Except that he isn't moving. Suddenly Mickey's brother Skinny comes screeching around the corner, the fat around his midriff bouncing up and down. He drops like a stone beside Mickey and begins wailing at the top of his voice. The sound is almost as shocking as the body of his brother. The Atkins never cried, not ever.

Mrs Atkin managed to scratch up enough money to give Mickey a decent send off. Fred J. Potter and Son arranged the funeral. Fred J. Potter attended our church. I never knew whether he was the original or the son. After Sunday mass he'd stand around in the church yard smoking cigarettes with other male members of the congregation. I used to look at his nicotine-stained fingers and imagine them preparing bodies for burial. He had a huge black hearse with 'Fred J. Potter and Son – Funeral Directors' inscribed in gold lettering along the sides, which he drove everywhere because it was the only vehicle he owned. Even when it was empty, it gave me the creeps.

The funeral cortège passed our school the following Thursday on its way to the cemetery. The hearse was driven very slowly, as though it only had one gear. Despite the admonitions of our teacher, the aptly named Mr Wilde (we had a lay teacher, not a member of the clergy, that year), we all rushed to the window to take a look. It was hard to imagine Mickey Atkin lying in the teak casket covered in flowers. I was willing to bet that was the closest Mickey had ever come to flowers.

The following week, the hearse passed the school again. This time, the casket was white. It was also considerably smaller than the one that had taken Mickey to his final resting place under a pepper tree in the Broken Hill cemetery. It contained the body of Teresita Stramandinoli, who had died of leukaemia. Her brother Santo was in the class above ours. He was fat and a bit of an outcast because he didn't speak much English. Teresita had been fat, too, before she got sick. No one rushed to the window to see her passing by.

When I got home from school that afternoon a council truck was parked at the bottom of the Nichol Street hill. Four council workers were erecting a barrier across the road. The barrier carried a sign that read 'Road Closed'.

RABBITO

Every Thursday afternoon, old Len Hutton rode his rusty pushbike up and down the neighbourhood streets. He would prop it carefully against someone's fence near the corner of a block and then walk the block, a hessian sack thrown over his shoulder. He walked with slow, measured steps. Why should he hurry, even if he could? His back was hunched, although this had little to do with the weight of the hessian sack. From time to time, you would see him up at the shops without the hessian bag over his shoulder, and his stoop would be just the same.

As he made his way up the street, he knocked on the back door of each house in turn. Everyone went round the back. Well, almost everyone. The doctor knocked on the front door when you needed him, as did the police, whether you needed them or not. And the travelling salesman from Adelaide who sold household appliances from the back of his car.

If someone answered the door, Len would reach into the sack and produce a pair of rabbits. They were already cleaned and dressed, and had the colour of newborn babies. Len would hold them up, gurgling and twisting his mouth into grotesque shapes. Len was deaf and dumb. There were a few people like him around town. We called them 'dummies', although later on we discovered that we were supposed to call them 'mutes', which didn't sound any better. In fact, I thought it sounded worse. I'd rather be a dummy than a mute any day. Anyway, the noises that came out of his mouth were his attempt to communicate. I guess he couldn't hear himself. If he could, he'd have known that there wasn't much point to all that gurgling.

When we were small, we were scared of Len, even though he turned out to be harmless. The bigger kids in the street said that if he got you alone, he would steal you. A little boy had disappeared once years ago and was never seen again. Mrs Hannaford, two doors down, whose husband had done the same disappearing trick, although at a much older age, spread the story about Old Len and the little boy. So when Len came around, we'd cower away from him as though he had some kind of disease.

The person at the door, almost always the woman of the house, would either shake her head politely and close the door, or inspect the rabbits. If she liked what she saw, she'd disappear into the house and reappear a few minutes later with a handful of coins, which she would exchange for the rabbits. Now and then, one of his regulars would be waiting for him, money in hand, and the exchange would take place immediately. The money would disappear into the side pocket of the old corduroy coat that Len wore, winter and summer. He would proceed down one side of the street and back up the other, retrieve his bike, and pedal laboriously down to the next block. He'd continue on his round until he'd disposed of all his rabbits. Later, you could see him sitting on a bench outside the Hillside Hotel having a beer. If it happened to be payday, some of the regulars might shout him to a few more beers, which he accepted with a duck of his head. Then he's get on his bike and weave his way down the street.

———

One Thursday afternoon, Pete and I were sitting with our backs against the smooth bark of the ghost gum that stood on the corner of our street when Len came by and leaned his bike against our side fence as he always did. Mum was one of his regulars, and more often than not she'd take a pair of rabbits. She was one of the few people who knew how to cook them properly. The way she did them, they didn't taste dry and tough. She'd wrap them in a square of cotton cut from an old bedsheet that had outlived its usefulness, smear the rabbits liberally with dripping spooned from a jug that lived permanently at the back of the fridge, and then cook them in an electric frying pan, removing the lid from time to time to turn and baste them with more dripping and boiling water.

Pete and I had been discussing a problem: money, or rather the lack of it. In those days, as we teetered on the edge of puberty, our out-of-school problems were mostly about money. Soon we would add girls to the list, which compounded the money problem and proved what Mickey Finn's Old Man had to say about life when he'd had a few: 'Life', he used to say, 'It's all about huntin'. Ya' go huntin' money, ya' go huntin' pussy—and then you're dead.' He was a real philosopher, was Mickey's Old Man. He could say things like that and get away with it because he had no wife and had a lot of huntin' to do, although Mickey said his Old Man was all talk and no action. 'All tip and no iceberg' was how he put it.

The truth was that we were constantly in need of cash. We had reached that stage in our development when we suddenly realised that money mattered. Some of the kids around the neighbourhood whose dads earned good money —sons of contract miners, the doctor, and the local magistrate—got pocket money. Pocket money was an alien concept to us. We were filled with envy and not a little loathing when, on Saturday morning, the Austin kids would flaunt their ten shilling notes.

If we wanted something special such as a book or a hunting knife or a new back tyre for our bike, we had to find other means. Taking an after-school job delivering newspapers was one option. Shoplifting was another. Neither appealed to me. I had flirted with the idea of shoplifting until one day when I watched a classmate being frog-marched out of Woolworths by a local cop. When I wanted something, my strategy was to whine to my parents nonstop and hope that the object of my desire would eventually appear under the Christmas tree. (On the rare occasion when it did, the desire for the object had usually long since passed.)

Pete's solution? We'd become rabbitos. It was an ambitious, even an audacious plan, and one that created its own set of problems. We only had the vaguest idea of how to go about catching rabbits. Another major stumbling block was the fact that we had no traps to catch the rabbits. We wanted to catch rabbits to make money. To catch rabbits you needed traps. To buy traps you needed money. Some years later, when I came across the work of Joseph Heller, I realised that Pete and I had stumbled across the concept of catch-22 not long after Heller had given it a name. And it was a catch that Pete and I failed to resolve under the gum tree in Railwaytown on that late Autumn afternoon. Eventually we gave up and went our separate ways. Old Len would never know how close he had come to being put out of a job.

A few days later, Pete came up to me in the schoolyard. Although we had started our school lives together, Pete was now a year behind me, having missed several months of schooling through a serious illness. Because of this, the only time that we got to see each other during the school day was in the schoolyard.

Pete had found a solution to our problem. He had taken our dilemma to Boofhead Willis, who lived at the end of his street. Boofhead was older than us and was one of the few older boys around town who was prepared to talk to younger ones. That's mainly because no-one his own age would talk to him. He was as ugly as hell, with a large arse and a face that was constantly exploding with pimples. But he had rabbit traps—lots of them. He'd inherited them from his father, who had been a semi-professional trapper before he got tired of life and blew his head off one day. One more sad soul helping Broken Hill maintain its place as the suicide capital of the country. Most adults kept at least one shotgun and a couple of rifles under the marital bed, so for them the problem of life had a ready solution.

Boofhead might have been ugly and unpopular. He might have been a shingle short upstairs. He might have been two school grades behind boys his own age. But he had traps. It also turned out that he had rat cunning. He struck a deal with us: He would rent us four traps—two each. For every two rabbits we caught, we would give him one. New traps cost five shillings, the same as a pair of rabbits.

'So', said Pete, whose arithmetic skills were on a par with mine, 'when we've caught twelve rabbits, we'll have enough money to pay Boofhead back and buy four traps of our own.'

This seemed reasonable. How hard could it be to catch twelve rabbits? The bush was crawling with them. Many people considered them vermin. The government introduced diseases in an effort to wipe them out. Miners who had access to explosives blew up their warrens with gelignite. Nothing worked. You had to practically brush them out of the way in order to set your traps.

One afternoon, once the deal had been struck, Boofhead led us into the sand dune behind Pete's house and showed us how to set a rabbit trap. It didn't seem all that complicated. When the trap was set, the main thing to avoid was losing a finger. Boofhead waggled the stump of the little finger on his left hand. He had lost the first joint to the jaws of a trap when he was eight.

There were several abandoned rabbit holes in the sand dune behind Pete's house. They hardly constituted a warren, and we weren't sure whether they had been dug by rabbits that had been kicked out of their colony for breaking some rabbit rule or other. It seemed odd to think of rabbits having rules of law, but you never knew.

Over the coming years, as I pursued them, first by trap and then by gun, I came to realise that the creatures might look dumb, but they were as cunning as hell. We knew that the holes were abandoned because Boofhead told us. He knew because of the absence of fresh rabbit pellets. 'This shit ain't fresh', he said, picking up a pellet and crumbling it to dust between his fingers. We nodded, pleased to be picking up rabbit trapping lore from Boofhead. 'Even when ya find an active warren, ya need to set yer traps in holes that are still bein' used. Not all them holes will be active, see. Some will be taken over by snakes or wild cats. Ya wanna be carful of them holes. Ya won't catch a rabbit and ya might even get yerself bit. Ya don't wanna get yerself bit.'

No, we certainly didn't wanna get ourselves bit.

Boofhead dumps the hessian bag containing a tomahawk and four soon-to-be-rented traps in the sand next to one of the holes. He scrapes at the sand in the long run up to the hole until the underlying clay is revealed. Picking up his tomahawk, he crafts a miniature coffin-shaped rectangle in the clay. The clay is harder than the sand but crumbles away easily enough under the blade of the tomahawk. He tries it for size against one of the traps, enlarges the head of the rectangle slightly, and then hammers the metal spike attached to the end of the trap through the sand and into the clay. He shows us how to angle the spike several degrees off vertical away from the entrance to the hole. This would provide enough resistance, preventing the rabbit from pulling the trap free and into the depths of the burrow where the trap would be lost for good along with the rabbit.

It was important for the rabbit to be able to get a certain way into the hole so it couldn't be poached by one of the feral cats that roamed the semi-desert. These brutish creatures, bred originally from domesticated cats that had escaped into the wild, knew no fear. They could tear a rabbit to pieces in a matter of seconds, and if cornered, had no hesitation in trying to do the same to humans.

Having secured the spike, to his satisfaction, Boofhead sets the trap. He does this by setting it on a firm piece of ground and depressing the spring with his foot. As he does so, the steel jaws yawn wide. Gingerly working his index finger under the leading edge of one of the jaws, he raises the steel plate and flips a small grooved hinge into place. This holds open the jaws with their serrated teeth. They'll stay that way until released by downward pressure on the plate—either by the foot of a rabbit or a careless hand. Then they'll snap shut with a sickening *clunk*. Boofhead gives us fair warning by touching the plate with a dry twig, which shatters into a dozen pieces. He shows us how he has filed down the tongue so that it only just secures the jaws. The slightest touch will set off the trap. 'Damn cunnin', them rabbits', he says, clicking his tongue in annoyance and admiration. 'Some of 'em can run right over a trap if the plate's too stiff. But no fuckin' rabbit ever ran over one of my traps, I can tell yer that.'

He sets the trap again. We watch, spellbound, as this ugly, pimpled, unloved lout caresses the trap, places it gently —caringly, almost—into the shallow grave that he has scratched out with his tomahawk. He inspects the placement carefully, his nose so close to the steel jaws that we hold our breath, points out the space that's needed underneath the steel trigger plate.

'If there ain't enough space the trap ain't gunna spring. The sand is gunna stop it springin'. Get it?'

We get it.

He takes a handful of sand and begins to bury the handle of the trap, trickling the sand up to the ugly jaws, carefully plucking out small pebbles, twigs, and hardened lumps of clay.

'If a lump of clay rolls under the plate, it ain't gonna spring. If they get between the jaws, the rabbit's gunna pull hisself out. They wanna live just as much as we do. You think they're just dumb, but they ain't. they're real cunnin'.' It's clear that Boofhead has a strange kind of love-hate relationship with his victims.

The most delicate part of the whole procedure is covering the jaws. Over these he places a square of newspaper, cut so it just covers the jaws and plate with an inch to spare all round, and then painstakingly sprinkles the softest sand he can find over the paper. Then he takes a long straight twig and removes all but the finest film of sand from the plate.

We're mesmerised by this performance. Boofhead is surgical in his movements. Even though he must have set a thousand traps, he sets this one as though it's his first. When the trap is completely covered, he scuffs the surrounding sand and lays a trail of old rabbit droppings up to the now invisible jaws.

After admiring his artistry for a minute, Boofhead pulls off a piece of saltbush and touches a spot in the centre of the plate. We jump back at the savagery with which the trap explodes, spraying sand and shreds of paper around the now-exposed trap.

'If ya get lucky enough to catch something', he says, 'make sure ya clean up afterwards. If them rabbits see even the tiniest bit of paper, they'll never come back to that hole.' He shakes his head and repeats the message in case we didn't get it the first time. 'Real cunnin', that's for sure. People talk about rat cunnin'. Rats got nuthin' on rabbits.'

Then he invites Pete to have a go at resetting the trap, coaching him along the way.

'You ain't left enough space under the plate.'

'That bit of clay there—that'll get between the jaws.'

'Gotta cover that little corner of paper.'

And when Pete has finished and stands back so that we can admire his work: 'It's too fuckin' neat. Anyone from a mile off can see there's a trap right there.'

Standing a couple of feet away, it looks perfect to me. Clearly I'm not anyone. Pete gets to work again, scuffing up the sand and scattered twigs and droppings around the trap.

When he's finished, he stands back grinning. I'm full of admiration. Boofhead shakes his head and demonstrated the inadequacy of Pete's work by whacking at the plate with a stick. The trap goes off, but sluggishly—not with the clean, crisp snap of Boofhead's trap.

'You'll never catch anything with a setting like that. Too much sand on the plate. Rabbits'll run right over it.'

Pete's face is beetroot red. But his eyes have a deter-mined look. Boofhead gets on his bike. After his fat bum has wobbled over the sand dune, Pete turns back to the trap. He works at mastering the art of trap setting until the sun goes down. I go home and do my homework.

On Thursday afternoon, Pete decides that it's time for out first foray into the bush with our traps. He's been prac-ticing all week and, with the help of Lanky Richards, who lives down the road at the abattoir, has filed down the safety catch that holds the plate on his traps. They're now as sensitive as the one Boofhead used to teach us how to set traps. The slightest touch will set them off. In evidence, he shows me a cut and bruising in the fleshy pad of his left hand, just below the little finger. 'Lucky it got me there', says Pete, ever the optimist. 'Bit higher and it would have taken the tip of my finger off.' Later, as our confidence and bravado grew, we'd have jousting matches with loaded traps.

———

Winter is coming on, and the late afternoon sun is already losing its sting as we sling the hessian bag containing our traps, tomahawk, sheets of paper, skinning knife, and torch over the handlebar of our bike and head west into the watery afternoon light. Lanky has given Pete the location of a promising warren two hundred yards west of the abattoir. What Lanky doesn't know about the bush isn't worth knowing. He graduated long ago from trapping rabbits and now picks them off, along with anything else that moves, with a battered .22 rifle that his dad handed down to him.

Following Lanky's directions, we turn left off the road to White's Pig Farm and on to a dirt track that skirts the abattoir. We follow the track over a low ridge. Looking back over my shoulder, all I can see of the town are the purple skimp dumps on the horizon.

The dirt track peters out. 'Should be over there.' Pete waves his hand towards a lone acacia tree some way off. We dump our bikes under the tree, and, taking our hessian bags in hand, trudge off through the low scrub.

The warren is just where Lanky had said it would be, set hard against a small clay-pan. There are about fifteen holes in all. 'Careful where you put your feet', says Pete. Having spent all week perfecting the art of setting traps, he is now the self-appointed expert on all aspects of catching rabbits, even though he has yet to snare one himself.

'These four', he says authoritatively, pointing to some holes at the southern edge of the warren.

'Why these four?'

'Look at the runs and all the fresh shit. These are the ones that are used the most. The others might be used by snakes.'

He probably made that up, but I'm not going to argue. I had no way of knowing it then, but Pete was on the road to become quite an accomplished bushman.

We set to work. Pete quickly finishes setting his two traps, and stands over me as I struggle with my own. It's scary holding the square of paper over the jaws and sprinkling on the sand. When the paper is well covered, I take a twig and carefully brush the excess sand off the plate area until the paper is covered by only the thinnest film of sand. Just the way Boofhead showed us.

When I've finished, and stand back, pleased with my effort, Pete looks over and says, 'Probably you wanna do that one again.'

'Why?'

'I don't think you left enough space under the plate.'

'I think I did.'

'Didn't.'

'Did.'

To prove his point, Pete picks up a dry twig and prods a spot in the sand above the plate. Nothing happens. Embarrassed and angry, I fish in the sand for the chain, pull the trap out of its sandy grave, and start all over again.

As a peace offering, Pete sets my other trap while I redo the first one. By the time we've finished, the sun has disappeared below the horizon. We ride home in silence through the darkening streets, anticipating the reward for our work.

The alarm clock explodes under the covers at four o'clock in the morning. I groan and turn over. In the wee small hours, the temperature has dipped below freezing, and the tip of my nose burns with cold. Hunched under the covers in the other bed, my little brother whimpers in his sleep. When I get out of bed, my feet stick to the freezing linoleum. In the bathroom, I dip a hand into the basin and rub the sleep from my eyes. Then I dress quickly, pulling on a down jacket, knitted beanie, and pair of gloves. A floorboard gives a sharp crack as I cross the lounge room and leave the house. Apart from the sharp retort from the floorboard, the house is silent.

The streets are silent too. Only Mick the Milko is up and about. These are the days before bottled milk. If you want fresh milk (and who doesn't?), you leave a pail hanging on the fence with a note inside it indicating how much milk you want. Mick the Milko ladles the required number of pints into the pail and hangs it back on the fence. The first person up and about in the morning fetches the pail and, as these are pre-pasteurization days, gives the milk a slow boil. The result is drinkable milk and a thick crust of yellow cream that will eventually find its way to the table along with the last of the summer fruit.

Seeing me, Mick gives a cheery wave. You have to be the cheery type to do this pre-dawn, door-to-door stuff. The milko, the baker, the postman, the traveling salesmen selling cleaning supplies and nifty household appliances are all cheerful, even at the end of the week, even when you don't have money to settle your account. If you're out of work, the money you owe goes on the never-never account. There's no questioned of being denied the goods that you and your family need just because you don't have the money to pay for them. The account is called the never-never, because the merchants, while living in hope, have already written off your debt.

I wave back to Mick and turn the corner into Pete's street. Pete is waiting for me on the corner, his lanky leg slung over the saddle of his bike, the corner street light showing up his face, which like mine is chapped from the biting pre-dawn breeze. As we ride out past the abattoir and turn left onto the dirt track leading to the warren, we take bets on the number of rabbits that will be trembling in our traps. Pete, always the optimist, thinks we'll snare four, for sure. We've followed Boofhead's instructions to the letter, so why wouldn't we? I'd happily settle for two.

Overhead, the stars are out, so bright that you could read a comic by them. Now and then, one streaks towards the horizon and disappears. Falling stars, we call them, although in school we learned that they aren't stars at all but meteors and bits of space junk burning up in the earth's atmosphere. We still call them falling stars. It sounds better.

Even though we've retraced our route exactly, it takes some time to find the warren. With mounting excitement, we drop our bikes and walk in ever expanding circles until we find it. Boofhead has warned us to approach with care. If they hear us, trapped rabbits can pull themselves and the trap into the depths of their hole. If that happens, it will be the last you'll ever see of your trap.

Finally, we find the holes where just a few short hours before we had so carefully laid the traps. Pete sprays torchlight around the holes. We both stare in disbelief. The scene is exactly as we had left it the previous afternoon. One hole has scuff marks where a lucky rabbit has skirted the trap. Apart from that, nothing has changed.

I want to leave the traps as they are. It seems such a waste of effort to pull them up, but Boofhead had been insistent. 'If youse don't catch anything don't leave the traps. They might get nicked. Anyway, twigs 'n shit'll blow over 'em, so you won't catch anything the second night. And make sure you leave the runs just the way they were.' We do as we were told.

We cycle home into the face of the rising sun. As the sun comes up, the wind picks up. Mean and bitter. Pete has come out without a beanie and the only thing he catches that morning is a chilblain—a kind of frostbite on the ear. They're not a good idea to catch, although sooner or later everybody does. The edge of the ear goes hard, and they're excruciatingly painful to touch. A popular sport in the school yard is to spot someone with a chilblain, sneak up behind them, and give it a flick.

Back home, I sling the hessian bag containing my two useless traps, tomahawk, and torch into the bike shed in disgust. Mum is fetching the milk pail from the side fence.

'How did you go?' she asks, seeing me empty handed, and then laughs. 'I hope Old Len does better than you.' I wonder how Len, so ancient and stooped that he can barely mount and dismount his bike, can possibly do all the hard work involved in trapping rabbits. Only later do I learn that he hasn't trapped for years. He gets his supply of rabbits from other trappers and sells them on commission.

In all of the excitement and then disappointment of rabbit trapping, I forget to do my homework. Dead tired, I drag myself to school and ask little priggish Leo, who sits behind me, if I can copy his.

'I didn't do it,' he smirks. 'It's First Friday. And I wouldn't let you copy if I did.'

You're in trouble.'

I hiss the usual threat at him. 'Just wait till recess, you little shit. You're a goner!'

Leo, whose dad owns a menswear store down Argent Street, never liked me much. The feeling was mutual. We became sworn enemies one day when Brother Viator caught me whispering and threw a wooden-backed board cleaner at me. I ducked, and the cleaner got little Leo right between the eyes. The rest of the class thought it was hilarious, but not Leo. Concussed, he staggered out of his seat, vomited on the floor, and then passed out. He disappeared for the rest of the week, and there was some muttering about legal action against the school.

I'd forgotten that it's the first Friday of the month. If you go to Mass on First Friday, you're excused from homework. This makes no logical sense, but I'm slowly beginning to realise that there isn't much about the Church that makes a lot of sense. If you manage to attend nine First Friday masses in a row, you're guaranteed a place in heaven —the Pope said so. Excusing us from homework is a straight-out bribe on the part of the Brothers to excuse them from the hard work of marking homework, and the even harder work of saving our souls.

The first thing that Brother Viator does on entering the room is to tell those who haven't been to First Friday Mass to hand in their homework. He looks at me, knowing how lax I am about First Friday Mass. I do go occasionally, but not often enough to save my soul.

'I went to Mass', I say.

'I didn't see you', says little Leo, immediately. I make a mental note to put a thumb tack on his seat during the morning break.

'Get out here', says Brother Viator, picking up the heavy leather strap from his desk.

'I ... I went down the South', I reply.

'Don't lie. Just get out here.'

Then Andrew Chappell, one of the South kids, saves my skin. 'He was there Bro', I saw him.'

Brother Viator gives Andrew a suspicious look, but there's nothing that he can do. I give Andrew a look of gratitude. Did he really imagine that he saw me at Mass? Well, I wasn't going to complain.

During the break, Pete and I are kicking a football back and forth across the schoolyard when Boofhead comes up to us. Normally, we wouldn't take any notice of him, but he's our business partner now, so we don't have much choice. Some of the other kids look at us. Normally, you wouldn't want anyone thinking Boofhead was a friend, but Pete is popular in the schoolyard, so no one says anything.

'How did youse go?' asks Boofhead. He has this leer on his face, but that doesn't mean anything. It's just the way his face is built.

'All right', replies Pete.

'So how many little bunnies, you get?'

'None', I say.

The leer broadens. 'Didn't think youse would. You never do the first time. Takes a while to get the hang of it. But make sure you look after them traps.'

'We'll go again tonight', says Pete.

'Good on yers!'

'Fuck off, Boofhead', I say loud enough for the other kids to hear.

'Gunna take you a while to pay off them traps, I reckon', says Boofhead before laughing and swaggering away.

That night, we do have more luck—just. In one of Pete's traps is a little kitten. For some reason that's what baby rabbits are called. It's so small that all four feet are caught in the trap. It starts quivering all over as we approach the hole, its eyes popping out of its head.

'Too bloody small', says Pete, disappointed. He pulls the pin out of the ground, takes the kitten by the scruff of the neck, steps on the hinge, and releases it from the trap. Its four broken legs dangle uselessly. Pete rings its neck and throws the limp body into the bushes.

———

Over the next few weeks, we start to have more luck, although Pete has more than I do. Some mornings we arrive at the warren to find that he has two rabbits while I have none. To be honest, when I see that my traps are unsprung, it doesn't really bother me; not like it bothers Pete. 'We're never going to pay off the traps', he says.

But it saves me the bother of killing, skinning, and cleaning the rabbits. I don't much like the stink of warm intestines and shit. And I don't much care for the smell of blood on my hands. I pack up my traps and smoke a cigarette while Pete dispatches his rabbits. Then we ride back to town where Pete skins and dresses his rabbits.

It takes me a while to get the hang of killing rabbits, although the procedure isn't all that complicated. They kick like hell when you pick them up by the back legs, particularly the bigger bucks. Well, you would too, if you knew what was going to happen to you. You place your thumb and forefinger around the rabbit's neck, and jerk downwards until you hear a crack. The rabbit goes limp, and that's the end of it.

The first time I tried it, I heard the *crack* and dropped the rabbit onto the hessian bag that held my traps and tomahawk. He lay there for a second or two, and then jumped up and ran off into the bushes. Apparently I hadn't done it hard enough. Pete thought it was as funny as hell, and rolled around on the ground, laughing his head off. I didn't think it was all that funny.

Once it's good and dead, you have to skin and gut the rabbit. To skin it, you slit the fur between its back legs and its arse, and pull the fur down over the rabbit's body just as if you're taking off a sweater. Then you just cut of the head and forepaws. You need to squeeze the piss bag empty before you slit it open so you don't get rabbit piss all over yourself. The guts come out all in one piece, warm and smelly. Then you poke your fingers through the membrane that separates the stomach sac from the lights, and pull out the lungs and heart. The only bits you leave are the kidneys. People like the kidneys for some reason, according to Boofhead. I don't know why. They don't look as though they'd be much of a feed, those little purple olives attached to the inner sides of the rabbit.

Pete knows that I don't like rabbit guts, so one day he pulls out a handful and throws them in my direction. I don't think he meant to hit me, but I look up at the wrong moment and the steaming entrails him me full in the face. I finished cleaning the rabbit I as working on, and throw the guts at Pete. They hit him on the back of the neck. Not as good as getting him in the face, but pretty satisfying all the same.

This is our first and only rabbit-guts fight. When we go

into the kitchen to clean up and get a cup of tea, we're both covered in blood and guts. His mum thinks we've been in a road accident and almost faints.

We store the rabbits in Pete's mum's freezer until we have four pairs, and then one Friday afternoon, we ride around the neighbourhood trying to sell them. Boofhead had told us that we'd have more luck with the housewives towards the end of the week before the men bought their pay packets home. Once the pay packet arrives, they spurn rabbits and head off to the butcher for slabs of steak and sides of lamb.

We thought that selling the rabbits would be the easy part, but we were wrong. Most of the women in the neighbourhood were loyal to Old Len and shut the door in our faces when they knew what we were up to. We even tried undercutting him by reducing the price to four shillings a pair. A few women fell for that one, but not too many. And it messed up our business plan with Boofhead. We ended up selling most of our catch to our mothers and aunties.

It never occurred to me that moving in on old Len's patch was morally questionable. As far as we were concerned, our financial needs were as great as his. Then one day, I found myself riding down the laneway behind his house. His little corrugated iron house was smaller, older, and more beaten up than all the other houses in the street. It wasn't much more than a shed, really, with lumps of rock holding down loose sheets of roofing iron.

I liked riding down the laneways and looking over fences. You saw all sorts of interesting things. One this day, when I looked into Len's backyard, I saw him sitting in the dirt chopping wood. He held the axe handle high up, near the throat. I guess he was no longer strong enough to stand up and take a decent swing at the blocks of wood. As I paused, he looked up. He squinted, and then when he noticed me staring at him over the fence, shook his fist. I'm not sure why he did that. Looking over fences was what people used to do back then before there was television.

———

It's dusk, and the sun is setting under a dirty sky when I get back from setting the traps. It looks like we're in for some overnight rain, which will make all of my hard work a waste of time. Pete is laid up in bed with an earache that will eventually land him in hospital, so I have to go alone. It's no fun being a rabbito without a mate. To be honest, I'd rather be lying on my bed reading a book. The idea of having to get up at four in the morning and push my bike into a bitter wind and stinging rain all alone doesn't thrill me at all. I'd been pretty careless in setting the traps because I wanted to get home and out of the cold. The possibility of catching anything other than a rabbit dying of myxomatosis was pretty slim.

I shove my bike into the back of the shed and dump the hessian bag containing squares of newspaper, my tomahawk, hunting knife, and torch under the workbench that holds Dad's tools. He likes tidiness. And cleanliness. 'Cleanliness is next to Godliness', he used to say, even though he didn't believe in God. He had this stock of clichés and would trot them out when he was in a good mood. It was his way of getting a conversation started. All we had to say was 'Yeah'. End of conversation.

Darkness closes quickly. I pick my way down the path towards the back of the house. There's a light in the corridor that runs through the centre of the house, but the kitchen and living room are in darkness. I guess that Mum and Dad are still at the pub. There's a faint light shining from the front bedroom. My sister would be in there playing with her dolls. She could spend hours in her room by herself doing god knows what with her toys. Or praying. Or doing whatever else it is that girls do. They were a complete mystery to me, and having one under the same roof did nothing to demystify them.

In the kitchen, I switch on the light. It's even colder inside than out, so I switch on the two-bar radiator and light the fire that's already been set. We're not supposed to use the radiator because of the cost, but we always do when out parents are out. I'll switch it off when I hear their car in the side street.

I wash my hands in the kitchen sink, make a cheese and jam sandwich, and am just about to take a bite when there's the sound of rubber on the road and a faint *Thump!* Two seconds later little Margie comes thundering down the corridor and into the kitchen.

'I saw it, I saw it', she says, trembling with excitement, the way she does when something significant happens in her life. 'I was looking out the window and I saw it.'

'Saw what?'

'The car hit a thing.'

'What kind of a thing?' I want to finish my sandwich, change my sweater and jacket that smell of dead rabbits, and sit in front of the fire that is now beginning to warm the kitchen.

'A thingy thing. It was dark outside. I was sitting in my room looking out of my window. I was waiting for Mum and Dad to come home. I'm hungry.'

'What happened to the car?'

'I dunno. It went away. It hit a thing. It made a squidgy sound. Maybe a horse. Maybe a kangaroo.'

We walk through to the front of the house. The street lamp on the corner has come on. There is a dark lump of something on the road. Neighbours, their evening meal interrupted, emerge from their houses. They stand around the dark lump on the side of the road. A car rolls down the hill, slows, and comes to a stop. Its headlights gleam on the dark lump.

'Poor old bugger', says Johnny, the plumber's mate from down the road.

'I was waitin' for me rabbits', says Doris from across the street.

'Well, you'll be waitin' a while now', says Johnny, the plumber's mate.

'I'm cold', says Margie. 'I want my tea. Where are Mum and Dad? They should be home by now.'

'Let's go inside', I say.

Some people drift away, but then rush back into the street when the police and ambulance arrive to load Len onto a stretcher and take him away. Not me. I stay in the kitchen, chewing on my cheese and plum jam sandwich.

————

Old Len's death means that the rabbito market is ours for the taking. But it's at about this time that we lose interest. With or without competition from Len, being a rabbito is just too much like hard work. Pete has ploughed all of his profits into buying traps and now has a substantial collection. Taking his cue from Boofhead, he rents them out to newcomers at the game. Being smarter than Boofhead, he also charges the newcomers for lessons on where and how to set the traps and other tricks of the trade. I sell my traps to one of the young kids from up the street and show him for free how to set them without losing a finger.

Years later, the government, in its wisdom, decides to ban the trapping of rabbits. This pleases the rabbits, and they begin to proliferate even more enthusiastically. Pete's traps become museum pieces, and our hard-earned knowledge and trapping skills become useless. Although we were only dimly aware of it at the time, in a few short years the mines would falter and fail, and the mining lore that went with them would also be lost for good.

WHATEVER HAPPENED TO MINTIE?

The short street beside our house ran up over the steep hill that had caused so much grief. The block on the opposite corner had once contained heavy earth-moving equipment belonging to Radford's Construction Company. The construction company sold it to the Methodists, who built an ugly, modernist church on the site. On Saturdays our quiet corner of town was cluttered up with wedding parties, and by the end of the day our front yard was covered in confetti. On Sunday mornings, the Holy Rollers would arrive. Dad, who had no truck with religion, would compete with the organ and the choir by carrying out chores such as hammering nails into the side fence.

One day he decided to blow up a lump of rock in the back yard with a stick of gelignite. The rock was impeding the march of concrete paving across the yard. He overdid the gelignite. The rock was blown to smithereens, and several fist-sized lumps shattered the stained glass windows of the church. Fearing an invasion of atheists, the parishioners rushed out of the church. When they realised what had happened, they crossed the road and glared at Dad over the fence. Dad merely turned his back on them and went on cleaning up the yard.

Between the church and the hill sat a handful of houses. The last house in the street, in the shadow of the hill, belonged to Bonnie and Nev. Well, it didn't really belong to them; they just happened to live there. I think it belonged to one of Bev's uncles. It was a rambling old corrugated iron house with a high, bullnose verandah and a large backyard.

I liked hanging out at Bonnie and Nev's place. For a while it became my second home. I liked Bonnie in particular, but wasn't so sure about Nev. He was what my Mum called a smart aleck. He was thin as a whippet, with tattooed arms and a Hollywood cut. Looking back, I realise that I had a bit of a crush on Bonnie. She had plump, warm flesh that would one day run to fat, and she dressed in tight blouses and pedal-pushers that left very little to the imagination. Sometimes in hot weather she would get around the house in tiny shorts and a bra, leaving even less to the imagination. She had pink, smooth skin that kept her plumpness in check and long blonde hair that tumbled onto her shoulders.

Bonnie was the first person to treat me as an adult. She shared her cigarettes with me, let me play her records, and taught me how to drive. Now and then she would offer me a beer, because she didn't like to drink alone. But I didn't really like the taste of beer. Nev could drink all day without any noticeable effect, but Bonnie would get tipsy after a few. If Nev wasn't around, she would start to flirt. One day, she scared the hell out of me by hefting her ample breasts in my direction and inviting me to take a suck.

Bonnie must have been in her early twenties. Nev was

considerably older. He had an ex-wife who had run off to Melbourne with another man. Nev had gone after her, but he never got her back. According to Bonnie, there'd been another woman with a couple of his kids in the picture at the time. She still lived in Broken Hill, but at the other end of town. With a population of 40,000, the place was just big enough for the paths of rival women not to cross.

The day things fall apart for good for Bonnie and Nev is the hottest of the summer. We are in the grip of a heatwave. For five straight days, the temperature has climbed towards 110 degrees. At night it fails to fall much below 100. In the streets, people move slowly, fan themselves, and ask of no-one in particular when it is ever going to end.

My mother doesn't like me going up to Bonnie's place. She thinks they're common, which I guess they are. However, on this particular day, she says nothing. Perhaps is just too hot to argue.

Bonnie is in the kitchen, sprawling on the couch that is pushed up against the wall of the kitchen. A packet of cigarettes, a lighter, and an ashtray rest on a stool at her elbow. A magazine is in her lap. An evaporation air cooler clatters in the background. These machines make a lot of noise and spit drops of water into the room; this increases the humidity, but does nothing for the temperature.

'Can you believe this heat?' asks Bonnie as I come in through the back door.

I like the kitchen. It smells of sausages and toast—a warm, lived-in smell. The rest of the house is all right, but the kitchen is the centre of life. Bonnie and Nev spend virtually all of their time here. I guess they use the bedroom for sleeping and for sex; not that I'd know much about the sex. I did catch them at it once. I could see them on the lounge room floor when I came into the kitchen from the back verandah: I had a fleeting glimpse of Bonnie's naked curves and startling breasts as she leapt to her feet and ran for the safety of the bedroom.

She throws me the cigarettes and lighter.

'You want a drink? Pepsi?'

'No, it's OK. I'll just have a smoke, and then I have to go.'

'Where you going, love?' asks Bonnie. She called everybody 'love', so I didn't take it personally.

'Down to the Boy's Club. We're going to play some basketball.'

'Bit hot for that, isn't it?'

'Maybe.'

'Well, I have to go out to the pig farm later. If you wanna have a drive, be back here by twelve.'

'Good-oh.'

I finish my tumbler of water and stub out my cigarette. Then I stand up to go.

'Can you put a record on for me, love?' she says. 'Sorry, I can't be bothered getting up.'

'All right.' I want to get going, but I'm happy to do little things from Bonnie. She's kind and generous, but she's also lazy. Dirty clothes are heaped in a corner of the kitchen, and the sink is piled with dirty dishes. It's such a contrast to my own home, which Mum keeps spotless with incessant work.

'Which one?'

'Umm, maybe the Trini Lopez. Put on *Lemon Tree*.'

Bonnie is a bit old-fashioned in some ways—although not in other ways. She'll have none of the Beatles or the Rolling Stones, who are beginning to crash and burn the airwaves. The 60s rock revolution is in full swing, instilling fear and loathing in the older generation. However, Bonnie is slow to join. Elvis is her only concession, although she prefers Elvis the Crooner to Elvis the Pelvis. And Trini Lopez is her latest crush. Every time I drop by, Trini's voice, scratchy on the little portable player that Nev picked up somewhere, comes floating through the kitchen window. She plays *Trini Lopez Live at PJ's* until she wears it out, and then moves on to *Lemon Tree*. I don't care for Trini much, not that she ever seeks my opinion. I prefer Peter, Paul, and Mary, another favourite of hers.

I put the Lopez album on the turntable, drop the needle onto track two, and turn away from the reedy voice.

> *Lemon tree very pretty,*
> *And the lemon flower is sweet;*
> *But the fruit of the poor lemon*
> *Is impossible to eat.*

Bonnie lights another cigarette. The smoke makes a sighing sound when Bonnie exhales. The smoke comes out of her nose as well as her mouth, which I find a bit disgusting.

'I must get a decent player', she says. 'Nev was going to get me one for my birthday, but he never did.' She sighs again, this time without the smoke. Sighing is one of her things. 'He doesn't really like music much. Listens to a bit of Slim Dusty when he's in the mood, which isn't all that often. Anyway, all I got for my birthday was a cartoon of cigarettes and a night at the pub.' She pauses to reflect on her birthday and pouts. 'He smoked half the fags, and then we had a drunken fight. Brings he home and slaps me around. Some birthday present that was!'

She's getting herself into one of those moods, so I head for the door. As I push open the fly-screen door, she says, 'Oh, can you call Mintie for me? I haven't seen her all morning. I want my little dog.'

'OK.'

I say 'OK' a lot when I'm not at home, where my Dad has banned it. 'Damned Yankee expression!' He also hates 'Ya know.' For someone who hardly went to school, he's very fussy about language. I find it hard to get through a sentence without using 'ya know' several times. 'Everyone uses it, ya know.' 'If I knew, you wouldn't have to open your mouth', was his stock reply.

I go into the back yard, past the broken down ute with its engine parts scattered on a tarpaulin, past the outback dunny and the water cistern, past the drooping wisteria creeper expiring in the heat. The sun, relentless now, hits me between the shoulder blades.

'Mintie!' I call. 'Here, Mint! Come here, doggy.'

Beyond a line of washing that's been hanging there for days, Nev's kangaroo skins, fresh from the tanning drum that morning, are staked out on the ground to dry. Some are already beginning to curl at the edges. A fresh lot of skins has been loaded into the 44-gallon tanning drum. A crow dances on the back fence. It caws—an ugly, desolate sound —and gives me the evil eye.

'Mintie. Here, girl!'

I give up on the dog and retreat from the heat to the kitchen. Bonnie is scratching at a match that doesn't want to light. A cigarette hangs slackly from her lips. Her hair hangs in damp blonde ringlets on her shoulders.

'She's not around.'

'I wonder where she is?' says Bonnie. 'She's a Mummy's girl. Never goes anywhere without me.'

'Probably up on the hillside chasing rabbits.'

'Not this Mintie', says Bonnie. She calls all her dogs Mintie. This one is Mintie III. Same name, different dog, although they always look similar—small black-and-white mongrel spaniels. 'She's a timid little thing, my Mintie. Loves her Mummy and her Mummy loves her.' She tries again to light her cigarette, but the match breaks in half. She gives up and rests the unlit cigarette in the ashtray.

'Well, I'm going now', I say. It isn't the first time that one of her little dogs has disappeared. Dogs do that kind of thing in Broken Hill. 'I'll see you later.'

'All right, love. Don't forget, if you want to go for a drive, come back about lunch time. And you can bring your cousin if he wants to have a drive.'

A few months ago, Bonnie taught me and cousin Pete to drive. Her method was simple: She took us out to a corrugated back road, turned the wheel over to us, and climbed into the back seat with a can of beer. It was fine for Pete, who was long and lanky and got the hang of it almost at once. But I was short, and had trouble reaching the clutch. Eventually, by lifting my left buttock off the seat and sliding forward into a kind of crouch, I managed to reach the pedals. However, it took me a long time to learn how to change gears smoothly, and I'd kangaroo the car along the dirt track while Pete and Bonnie laughed at me. Eventually, when I too got the hang of it, Pete and I bickered over whose turn it was to drive.

———

The Boys' Club was run by the police. Its official name was the Police Boys Club. Some of the kids in the town avoided it because of is association with the law, although the only evidence of a link was a plain-clothes sergeant who managed the club and taught judo on Saturday morning. He didn't do much judo himself because of his weight. He didn't look much like a cop, but we knew he must be one because everyone called him 'Sarge'.

The Boys' Club had a boxing ring and two trampolines set in pits so that the beds were at ground level. Originally, they had been above ground. The problem with that arrangement was that if you jumped too high and missed the mat on your way down, you were likely to end up on the floor with a broken arm or leg. The problem with the new arrangement was that if you missed the mat, you were likely to end up with a broken neck.

The gym room had weights, parallel bars, roman rings, and a vaulting horse. It smelt of sweaty leather and dust—kind of masculine, when you come to think of it. Between the clubhouse and a dusty municipal park stood a basketball court. It wasn't much of a court. The tarmac was pitted and cracked, which made dribbling a lottery. At the back of the clubhouse was a football oval and a rifle range. And that was just about it, as far as sporting facilities were concerned. Not much, you might think, if you compare it to fancy fitness clubs today, but we appreciated it. Getting banned for a month, or, heaven forbid, for a year, for doing something stupid (well, for being caught doing something stupid) was about the worst thing that could happen to you. When Little Mickey was banned for life for setting fire to the vaulting horse we mourned for him. As far as we were concerned, that was worse than losing a parent. He hadn't really intended to set fire to the club; he'd just been fooling with a cigarette lighter like you do and things got out of hand.

I shove my bike into the rack and walk through the club house. Two smaller boys are sparring in the boxing ring under the supervision of the sergeant. One of them has a thin trickle of blood coming from his nose. The sergeant has sweat beads on his face and grey sweat stains under his armpits.

'How many times do I have to tell you to keep your guard up?' he shouts at the boy with the bleeding nose.

The boy hangs his head and wipes off the blood, leaving a dark streak on the back of his glove.

In the gym room, three boys are working out on the vaulting horse. They take turns running across the room, jumping onto the springboard, somersaulting over the horse, and landing on the padded mats on the other side. One misses his step and lands on his back, the air knocked out of him. That's the way it is at the Club—something is always happening, and it usually involves pain and blood. When someone gets hurt the Sarge says, 'Stop snivelling. My job is to make men out of you lot!'

Outside on the basketball court, Pete and three other kids are dribbling balls around the court and shooting baskets. They don't look all that enthusiastic. Pete's face is even redder than usual. When I come out of the clubhouse, Pete and two of the kids retreat to a shady patch near the building. These two, Russell and Georgie, go to the high school. Pete and I go to the Marist Brothers, so we only see them when we hang out on the street or go to the club. Russell is a bit of a bullshit artist. He has a round face and straight, greasy hair that flops in his eyes. He looks harmless enough and acts like a fool, but he has a terrible temper. I had a fight with him once and he just about killed me. Georgie is tall and thin and very quiet. His family come from Thessaloniki and own a shoe repair shop down the street from the Boys' Club.

Like Pete and me, the third kid goes to the Marist Brothers, or 'Marzies'. His name is Tony Glover, and he's a new kid in town. He's not like us, and will never be one of us. I don't mind him, although I'd never tell that to the others.

There he is, out there on the basketball court in the blazing sun, practicing his jump shots while we sit in the shade. His feet are shod in fancy new trainers, while we wear dirty Dunlop Volleys with split sides and fronts so worn down that our toes poke through. Our dads have ordinary jobs, or no jobs at all. Tony's dad is the local magistrate—Justice Glover, they call him in the newspaper. They recently arrived from Newcastle or some other impossibly remote city on the eastern seaboard, and have to move on every three years, so Tony never gets the chance to make good friends. We put up with him because he bribes us with his fancy possessions. Once he even lent Pete his ten-speed bike for the weekend. Right now his transistor radio is sitting on the edge of the court. Mick Jagger wails: *Hey, hey, you, you, get off of my cloud.* I'm not so sure about the Stones, but they're definitely preferable to Trini Lopez.

I go on to the court and snatch Tony's ball out of his hands. Anyone else would have snatched it back, but he just stands with his hands on his hips and watches while I dribbled up the sideline, shoot at the basket, and miss. I dribble down the other end. It's baking hot on the court, and the deep cracks in the bitumen make the ball shoot off at crazy angles.

Georgie comes and stands at the edge of the court. I pass him the ball. He props and pots a basket from thirty feet. He's a natural at all sports. If he was a boaster or bull-shit artist like Russell, he'd be hated, but because he's shy and doesn't say much, everyone admires him. I fetch the ball and drop kick it over towards the rifle range. Tony runs to retrieve it. Georgie and I go back to the shade, where Pete and Russell are debating what to do to cool off. None of us has enough money to get into the local swimming pool, so Russell suggest that we go to the skimp dumps where there's a dam. Pete thinks it's a good idea, but Georgie isn't so sure. The last time we went to the skimp dumps one of the mine security guards shot at us. The salt-petre pellets won't kill you, but they sting like hell if you cop a shot in the arse.

'Coming?' asks Pete.

'No, I don't think so. I have to go somewhere.'

'Where?'

'There's a lost dog in our street. I have to help find it.'

'Someone's baiting dogs around here right now', says Russell. 'It's probably been poisoned.'

'Well, anyway, I have to go.'

'Well, see ya', said Pete.

'See ya.'

———

Bonnie is still in the kitchen. She's no longer on the couch but has moved to the end of the long wooden table that occupied the middle of the room. She has taken a shower and changed into a pair of cut-off Levis and a blouse, both of which are a size too small.

She holds a mug of tea. A cigarette smoulders in the ashtray in front of her. From time to time she picks it up and flicks off the ash. She notices me looking at the mounds of her breasts struggling out of the top of her blouse and grins.

'How was it?' she asks.

'Hot.'

'Hot. Yeah. Too right it is! Where's your cousin?'

'He's doing something else.'

'Oh.' She looks thoughtful.

'Did Mintie come back?'

'No', she says, looking out of the window.

I wonder about Mintie. The little mongrel followed Bonnie around like a shadow day and night. Maybe Russell is right—maybe she'd picked up a bait, and was dying or already dead. Bonnie had got her after the last Mintie disappeared. That was the previous Guy Fawkes Night. They assumed that she had been spooked by the fireworks, run off, and had been unable to find her way back home. That last Mintie has been adventurous. This one was extremely timid. She would lurk at Bonnie's side, particularly when Nev was around, so she wouldn't get kicked.

I didn't mind this Mintie. She reminded me of the mongrel dog I'd had when I was a little kid. His name was Rusty, because of the colour of his hair. He disappeared one day too. I spent days riding all over town looking for him, but he never came back. I thought about him from time to time, and for a while kept a little black-and-white snapshot of him on the table in my bedroom where I did my homework. Eventually, like Rusty, the photo too disappeared.

Bonnie's dogs were definitely accident prone. One had been shot by Nev for nipping one of the neighbourhood kids on the arm. It was the dog's bad luck that Nev was at home when the kid's mum came across the road to complain. Bonnie tried to stop him, but he shook her off and loaded one of his rifles. She pleaded with him, but he said, 'Once a dog starts biting people, that's it.' He went out the back, shot the little dog through the head, and then went to the pub, leaving Bonnie to bury her pet near the back fence. When Nev came back from the pub, she had cleared out. After a couple of days, he tracked her down to a cousin's place out the South. She agreed to go back to him, but warned him never to touch her dogs again.

Nev had his own dogs: two lean, mean roo dogs. They went with him everywhere, but were never allowed in the house. Nev didn't approve of dogs in the house, and would look at Mintie in disgust when she leapt into Bonnie's lap for a pat and a cuddle. Bonnie didn't care what Nev thought. It was her house, after all, and if she wanted a dog inside, then she'd have a dog inside. Nev had to put up with it, but he smouldered and kicked out at Mintie if she ever came near him. Once, when Bonnie was out of the room, I saw him pick the dog up and throw her across the room— all because she'd been yapping at something, a mouse probably, behind the skirting board.

'Yap, yap, yap, yap, yap', said Nev, as Mintie got unsteadily to her feet and shook herself. She looked at him with baleful, spaniel eyes and disappeared behind the couch with her tail between her legs.

Nev was a first rate bushman. Everyone knew it. 'An arsehole', they said, 'but terrific in the bush.' He scraped a living by doing odd jobs at the Pig Farm, trapping rabbits and tanning and selling 'roo hides that were turned into eiderdowns. He was also a crack shot. He kept two rifles in the boot of his car—a .22 and a .303. He also had a shotgun that he took from his Dad when his Dad got put away. 'He won't need it where he's gone', said Nev. It was a beautiful piece with a carved stock. Nev kept it dismantled in a wooden case under the bed he shared with Bonnie. Once a week he took it out, cleaned and polished it, and then put it back under the bed. Now and then he took it up the river to shoot ducks.

I kept out of Nev's way, and in general he ignored me, except for some sarcastic teasing when he'd had a few drinks. There was only one time that he'd been nice to me. Pete and I were wagging school, because Pete hadn't done his homework and didn't want to get into trouble. (It never occurred to us that we'd get into much bigger trouble if the truant officer caught us.) We were in Dorian's bakery buying Cornish pasties for lunch. You could get them cheaply if you took the ones from the day before. We were just leaving the shop when Nev came in. He gave us the once over and then said, 'You blokes wanna come for a ride?'

Pete looked at the big black Customline pulled in to the kerb. 'Can I drive?' he asked. I would never have dared to ask such a question, but Pete had plenty of cheek.

'No, you can't', said Nev. He'd bought his car from a bushie who had gone broke in the drought, and it was his pride and joy. He let Bonnie drive it now and then, but only grudgingly. I held my breath, hoping that Pete wouldn't mention that the both of us had already driven it.

Nev bought a box of meat pies, and we went out into the street. I saw that Nev's two 'roo dogs were in the back of the car, so I immediately got into the front passenger seat, forcing Pete to ride in the back. We stopped at a pub for beer and Cokes, and then Nev drove to the gun shop at the end of Argent Street where he bought ammunition.

The 303 shells packed into their cardboard boxes were surprisingly heavy. Pete beat me back to the car and jumped into the front seat. I climbed reluctantly into the back. The dogs were about as happy to see me as I was to see them. One of them bared his ugly fangs at me and snarled. Nev told it to shut up, started the car, and drove out on to the Menindee Road. I wondered why Nev had offered to take us into the bush.

And I wondered why we had accepted.

About ten miles out of town, Nev turned onto a dirt road that snaked across the plains toward a line of low hills. Since leaving the outskirts of town, we had not see a single car. Nev drove like a gangster in the movies, his left hand caressing the steering wheel, a cigarette in his right. When he finished his cigarette, he flicked it out of the window and asked me to hand him a can of beer from the esky that was on the floor at my feet. 'There's an opener in the glove box,' he said to Pete. Pete passed me the opener. I opened a can of West End, which fizzed all over the floor of the car. I didn't say anything, but passed the can to Nev.

'Wrong time of day for 'roos', said Nev, slurping at the beer. 'Dawn or dusk is best—when they come out to feed. But we might see some euros up in the hills.'

For someone so proud of his car, he drove fast, fish-tailing through the bends and gunning it on the straight. The car was soon covered in fine red dust. A long plume of dust hung in the air behind us. It was a fine day, hot now that the sun was well up in the sky.

Before we entered the hills, Nev pulled over and took

two rifles out of the boot of the car. The dogs got excited and scratched at the back door, eager to get out. One of the guns was a 303, the other was a less powerful 22. He loaded them and handed the 22 to me and the 303 to Pete. I sat in the back seat, sulking at having been given the baby gun. Pete sat up front looking smug.

At the base of the range of hills, Nev stopped again and ordered Pete into the back of the car. When he opened the back door, the 'roo dogs jumped out and went tearing off into the scrub. Nev whistled at them until they came back and jumped into the front seat.

Pete and I sat in the back with our rifles sticking out of the window. Pete looked at me and grinned. 'This beats the shit out of school', he said. We both felt very grown up. I hoped that nothing would go wrong. I had this nervous feeling in my stomach. I guessed it was a grown-up kind of feeling. I thought of my mother and how disappointed she would be to know I was tearing around the scrub in a car with beer and loaded guns instead of sitting obediently in class practicing Latin declensions.

We drove for about twenty minutes before Nev said, 'Over there'. A euro bounded out of the hills on Pete's side of the car.

'Wait till it props', said Nev.

'Will he?' asked Pete.

'They always do. And it's a she, not a he.'

'How do you know?'

Nev ignored the question.

Just as he had said, the euro suddenly propped and looked back over its shoulder at the car.

'Now', said Nev.

Pete sighted the 'roo and squeezed the trigger.

'Fuck it!' he said. At the report of the gun, the euro had turned tail and bounded into the hills.

'Here', said Nev. 'You drive.' Pete and I looked at each other. Nev never let anyone else drive his car. Pete jumped quickly out of the car in case he changed his mind. Nev got in the back, cradling the 303 in one hand and his can of beer in the other. Pete drove cautiously. He didn't want anything to happen to the car. The road dipped through a gully and climbed the next ridge.

'Stop!' said Vic.

Although we were driving slowly, the car skidded in the cracker dust when Pete hit the brakes.

A Big Red had propped ahead of us and was looking back over its shoulder at the car. It was at least 150 yards away.

'Must be a good seven foot', said Nev. Despite the distance, he lined it up and dropped it with a head shot. Body shots were dicey, Nev had told us. If the 'roo was only wounded and retreated into the hills, you had to follow it on foot, sometimes for miles, to finish it off. You never left a wounded animal to suffer. Given some of the things that I'd heard about Nev and what he did to humans, I thought that this was a pretty funny attitude to have.

Pete and I leaned against the front of the car and ate our pasties while Nev and his dogs went after the 'roo. He skinned it and cut off its tail. Then he removed a fillet of lean flesh from its side, along with a couple of large hunks from its leg. He wrapped the raw skin and tail in Hessian sacking. Then he let the dogs tear the carcass to shreds.

Back at the car, he wrapped the lumps of meat in butchers' paper and placed them in the esky along with the beer.

Then he wiped the blood off his hands on a piece of rag and helped himself to another beer and a meat pie.

———

'So', says Bonnie, 'you want to come for a drive to the Pig Farm or what?' She seems a bit upset about something. I wonder if it's because I'm late. I see that she's no longer drinking tea, but has a can of beer sitting on the kitchen table.

'Well...'

'Nev needs his toolbox.'

My desire to drive the Ford and my desire not to go anywhere near Nev tugged at each other. 'I thought I might ...' My utterance petered out. I wasn't sure what I might ... .

Bonnie pick up her cigarettes and lighter. She looked at me and frowned. 'Suit yourself, love. But you don't have to worry. It's just ... I thought we might go for a bit of a drive afterwards. Out to Silverton, maybe.'

Once we're out past the abattoir, she stops the car. I run around to the driver's side, and she slides into the passenger's seat.

'Fag?'

I shake my head. Not right now. When Pete and I were young, we used to steal my aunt's cigarettes. She never seemed to notice. Smoking illicit cigarettes was dizzying and delicious. One day, when I'd just started going to Bonnie's place, she caught me filching one of her fags. All she said was, 'You don't have to sneak them. You want one? Just help yourself.' The cigarettes never tasted quite the same after that.

The road out to the Pig Farm is deeply rutted, as it's

rarely graded. You have to drive carefully, weaving the car from one side of the road to the other to avoid the deeper ruts. The corrugations make the car vibrate violently.

Just short of the Pig Farm, we change places again. It wouldn't do for Nev to catch me driving his precious car.

The Pig Farm stinks. On days that Nev works there, he comes home reeking of garbage. Bonnie didn't like the smell, and I didn't care much for the pigs in their pens covered in mud and slop. When the slops and garbage were poured into their troughs, they buried their whole faces into the greasy, rotting mess and snorted it up.

Nev comes across the yard and takes a metal toolbox from the trunk of the car. He has a cigarette hanging from his lower lip; it sticks there, burning lower and lower. Nev rolls his own cigarettes. He can do it with one hand. Bonnie and I get out of the car.

He looks me up and down. 'I see you brought your little poodle along for the ride', he says sarcastically. 'Where's your other little bitch?' For some reason, he thinks this is a funny thing to say, and snorts.

'Why do you always have to be such an arsehole, Nev? Can you tell me that?' She gives her cigarette a violent flick, and some of the ash lands on Nev's work boot.

He steps towards her and puts his face close to hers. 'Don't be lippy. Forgotten last night already, have ya? Like the same again tonight, would ya?'

Bonnie says nothing, but gives him a sullen look.

Nev picks up his toolbox and starts to walk away, then turns sharply and says, 'When you get home, turn the skins. They need to be turned.'

'I mightn't be going straight home.'

'Well, I don't want you running around town in my car.

Not with Lover Boy here. Not with anyone, for that matter.' He gives her hard stare. 'So, where you going?'

'Hairdresser's, maybe.'

'Hairdresser's, my arse! What? Got a hot date?' He gives another bitter little laugh. Bonnie says nothing.

'Well, just get those skins turned.'

'Turning the skins is your job.'

'Just do it, can you? I won't be home till late.'

'How come?'

'None of your business.'

'Well, don't get caught again.'

'Oh, up your arse!' says Nev.

'Yeah, that's the way you like it, isn't it? Nice and tight!?'

I wish she'd stop. Some of the other men in the yard are looking now. Maybe that's why she continues with her goading. He isn't going to do anything in front of his workmates.

'Just do the skins, will ya?'

'Maybe.'

'Lippy bitch!' He turns and walks back towards the workshop. There's a hole in the back of his jeans, and I can see his underpants.

'Up yours too', says Bonnie. Then under her breath: 'Faggot!' She turns to me. 'Get in, love.'

She reverses the car and guns it between the gateposts. We drive back past the abattoir, skirt the town on a side road, and swing left onto a bitumen road in the direction of the Mundi Mundi Plain. When we get to Silverton, she slows. All roads out of The Hill have a pub some way beyond the city limits, which puts them beyond the reach of liquor laws—not that the pubs in town take much notice of these. Some of these stand alone by the roadside. Others, like the Silverton Pub, are part of a small outback settlement.

Bonnie pulls the car nose-first into the verandah. Most outback pubs are built of corrugated iron, but this one is made of stone. Behind it stands the ruins of a much more substantial pub that had been built in the days when Silverton counted for something. It had burned down many years before.

Inside, it's cool and dim. Two men in broad-brimmed bushie's hats are talking to the barman.

'Well, look who's here', says the younger bushie. 'Eskimo Nell.'

I don't like the way he looks her up and down, but Bonnie doesn't seem to mind. 'I'm just here for a drink today, boys', she says, climbing onto a stool.

The barman pulls two beers and lines them up. Bonnie puts her cigarettes on the bar.

'Did you want a beer?' she asks me.

'Um, not really. Not right now. A Coke.' To be honest, I don't like the taste of beer, but I have one every now and then. Bonnie sometimes says she doesn't like to drink alone, but it never seems to stop her.

The barman goes to remove one of the beers, but Bonnie puts a hand on his arm. 'It's all right, Johnno', she says. 'I'll look after them.' I wonder when she's planning on going back to town to look for Mintie. That was supposed to be our mission for today.

Bonnie downs the beers quickly. She orders another with a whisky chaser and lights a cigarette. Then she starts talking to the two bushies on the other side of the bar. I take my Coke and sit on the verandah. It's hot. A mongrel dog lies curled up at the shady end. Apart from the dog, and the flies that keep circling my face, there's no sign of life.

When I go back into the bar, Bonnie and the younger bushie have disappeared. Her cigarettes, lighter, and unfinished beer are on the bar.

'You want another Coke?' asks the barman.

'Where is she?'

'She'll be back soon', says the older bushie and laughs. 'She has a little job to do. It won't take long.'

After about ten minutes, Bonnie and the younger bushie come in through a door on the other side of the bar. The younger bushie grins and winks as his mate. Bonnie's face is flushed, and she looks a bit unsteady on her feet. She finishes her beer and then says, 'All right, love. Better get back. Have to find my little dog.'

'You want me to ... ?' I go to pick up the keys.

'No, no, it's fine.'

We drive back to town, Bonnie weaving slightly from time to time. She pulls up in the middle of the lot at the front of the house. Her cheeks are wet. I didn't realise that she'd been crying.

'I'm just going to lie down for a while', she says. 'I'm a bit upset.'

'I think I'll ride the streets for a bit. See if I can find Mintie', I say, assuming the little dog's disappearance is the source of her tears.

'Thanks, love. You're a good kid.'

I don't want to be thought of as a good kid. I don't want to be thought of as a kid at all. I liked it better before, when we were having fun. I'd sensed for a while that something was coming apart but couldn't put my finger on it. Things were stirring in the adult world, and today they had become a whole lot worse. I shake my head. Maybe she's right—maybe it's because I'm still just a kid. She turns away, and then says over her shoulder, 'Oh, can you turn the skins before you go?'

'Sure.'

Bonnie walks up the steps to the front verandah and disappears into the house. I walk around to the back. The sun beats on my back. It's still hot, but the sun isn't as fierce as it was earlier in the afternoon. To the west, some clouds gather on the horizon. A change is on the way.

In the yard, the freshly tanned 'roo skins are staked out on the ground. The new skins are in a 44-gallon tanning drum. The outside of the drum is covered in rust. I pick up the broomstick and pushed down into the skins. I plunge the broomstick up and down to rotate the skins. It's hard, smelly work. As the bruised purple 'roo skins with their soft white undersides began to roll, a skin of a different hue rotates to the surface. It's a small shaggy white skin with patches of black. I drop the stick and leaned against the drum. Right then, Bonnie comes out of the back door and weaves her way towards me. She has a can of beer in one hand and a cigarette in the other. I want to tell her not to come any nearer, but say nothing. When she sees the skin, she drops her cigarette and puts her hand to her mouth.

When I call around the following afternoon, I find the place abandoned. The back door has been ripped off its hinges, and there is broken glass everywhere. When I walk into the back yard I see that the tanning drum has been overturned, and skins are lying in a jumbled mess on the ground.

Mrs Hubbard, the next door neighbour, is hanging over the side fence. She tells me what happened. 'Something shocking it was, love. He come home, late as usual, and drunk as usual. She was just as drunk. I seen her staggerin' around the backyard in the moonlight crying and holding onto the hide of that poor little dog of hers. As soon as he come home, she went for 'im. Started beltin' into 'im with a broomstick. But she weren't no match for 'im. She got in one good belt to the side of the head before 'e snatched the stick from 'er and gave 'er the hidin' of a lifetime. I though 'e was gunna kill 'er, but she got away and ran off up the lane. Then 'e set to smashin' up the place. Damn near wrecked it. Then 'e put some stuff in 'is car and drove away. That's the last I seen of 'em. Thank Gawd! This time I hope they never come back.'

THE LIBRARIAN

It wasn't yet Christmas, and the long summer holidays, so eagerly embraced at the beginning of December, lay ahead of me like a prison sentence. Terminal boredom arrived early that year, and I was almost looking forward to going back to school.

My friends (well, those with families who could afford it) had gone off to the beach. Most went to Adelaide, but some travelled further afield. Possibilities for entertainment were strictly limited. The municipal pool and the picture theatre cost money. Some kids got their kicks from shoplifting, a form of entertainment that was too risky for me, coward that I was. A less risky form of theft was raiding the neighbours' fruit trees. Looking back, I have no idea why we saw this as a form of amusement. The fruit rarely tasted good, and the green stone fruit gave us stomach aches. But at least we could wipe our conscience clean at Saturday afternoon confession. 'Bless me Father for I have sinned. I nicked six green nectarines from Mr McCartney's back yard.'

Instead of swimming and shoplifting, I got my kicks from reading. The problem was that I'd read everything that was worth reading in the kids' library, but officially wasn't old enough to join the adult library. On my third visit to the library in a week, I returned the books I'd finished overnight and asked Miss Moloney, the librarian in charge of the kids' library, if she had anything new for me. She shook her head.

'Sorry', she said. 'You read too quick.'

This struck me as an odd think for a librarian to say. 'Fuck it!' I thought. The words must have been written all over my face because she heaved herself out of the high-backed librarian's chair.

'Wait here', she said, and taking my library card form the desk, she crossed the corridor to the adult library. Five minutes later, she returned with a different card. She had exchanged my kid's card for adult membership to the library. 'Go and see Mr Vanderplank, he's expecting you', she said, handing me my new library card.

He's expecting me. If only I'd known how prophetic those words would turn out to be.

Although I never knew his name, I'd seen him around, collecting mail at the post office and shopping at the Service Stores. He carried his groceries in a woven wicker shopping basket just like our Mum's. And I knew that he was the senior librarian because I would sometimes glimpse him reshelving books and pottering around in the usually unoccupied senior library.

Card in hand, I waved Miss Moloney goodbye and crossed the corridor. One step closer to adulthood. There I handed my card to the elderly male librarian—who, I had just learned, was called Mr Vanderplank. He must have been in his mid- to late-50s, which in those days counted as elderly. He turned the card over in his hands, looked me up and down, blinked at me several times through his glasses that made his eyes look unnaturally large, gave me a thin smile, and slipped the card into a card-holder on his desk. When he said 'Welcome to the adult library', I detected a slight accent. Later, he told me that he was originally from the Netherlands, although he had lived in Australia for many years. *The Netherlands*. I turned the phrase over in my mind. It sounded very remote and very cold. He might as well have said he came from Mars. In geography, we'd been struggling with incomprehensible facts about the Ruhr Valley. I guessed he must have originated from somewhere around there. Well, at least I had an explanation for his odd dress sense and preference for women's shopping baskets.

The librarian was different. Not a good thing in Broken Hill in those days. Not a good thing to be different anywhere in rural Australia, come to that. Looking back, this strikes me as a paradox. Rural Australia was full of 'characters', none more so than Broken Hill. And 'characters' by definition were different. But you had to be different in the right sort of way; then you could get away with it. There were rules to being different. However, like all of the important rules of the game, these were never spelled out.

The librarian was definitely different in the wrong sort of way. It wasn't just his thick glasses; his pale, watery eyes; or the strangeness of his origins. It wasn't even his dress sense: tweed jacket (even though it was the height of summer), check shirt, and pale green tie that was knotted crookedly around his sagging neck. Nor was it the gingery hair going grey and curling around his collar, or the moustache and straggling goatee. It was his aura. In a few short years, the explanation would be straightforward: 'He just puts out a weird vibe, man.' However, I wasn't to learn that way of understanding and articulating the universe until I had escaped The Hill.

The library was a single large room at the front of the civic hall. It had a lofty ceiling and two arched windows that looked out onto the street. The floor was covered in thick olive-coloured linoleum that was soft to walk on. Several heavy wooden reading tables that smelled of beeswax occupied the centre of the room. The books were housed on shelves running around three sides of the room and stretching to the ceiling. Books on the higher shelves were reached with the help of a ladder.

I walked slowly around the shelves, getting a sense of their contents. The collection was divided into works of fiction, which were shelved in alphabetical order, and non-fiction, which were catalogued according to the Dewey decimal system. We had been taught the Dewey decimal system in school, but learning a system from a dog-eared handout and learning it by plucking books from a library shelf represented two radically different ways of learning. All at once I got it: This system of numbering and sub-numbering was a way of carving the universe into ever-smaller chunks, and assigning each chunk to its rightful place, as determined by Mr Dewey.

As a fully-fledged adult member of the library, I was entitled to borrow three books at a time and could keep them for up to two weeks. And, I could borrow any books I liked. In the fiction section, under 'C' I found several titles in *The Saint* series authored by Lesley Charteris. I pulled one off the shelf and took it to a reading table. Danny

Clark, the only other boy in my class who was a bit of a reader, had said *The Saint* books had sex in them. I scanned through the book but couldn't find anything remotely sexy. Maybe it needed a closer read. Despite the apparent absence of sex, I enjoyed the few pages I'd read, so I put the book aside to borrow later.

I was the only borrower in the library, and the Librarian didn't appear to have much to do. He sat behind his desk by the door and read a book. Several times I caught him looking at me. It kind of gave me the creeps, having those eyes follow me around the room, but I pretended not to notice. I guessed it was his job to keep an eye on me, to see that I didn't stick a gob of chewing gum under a reading table or stuff a book down my t-shirt.

In addition to the collection of *Saint* stories, I selected a book on big game hunting in Africa. I picked it mainly because of the dramatic photos of lions being slaughtered. My final pick was *The Guns of Navarone*, a wartime thriller by the Scottish author Alistair MacLean. This one I enjoyed, and over time I ended up reading most of MacLean's novels.

I took the books to the check-out desk. The librarian looked them over, nodding several times. I didn't know whether he approved of my choices or not. He stamped the return-by date in the back of each book, removed the cards from each book, put these along with my library card into a catalogue tray, and gave me another thin smile. All of his actions were slow and deliberate, as though he were performing the task of checking out a book for the first time. It seemed that he didn't want me to leave in a hurry. Being a librarian out in the middle of the bush must have been a lonely job.

I polished off those first three adult library books in a couple of days. They weren't the first three grown-up books that I'd read. My first foray into the word of adult literature occurred when I was eight, when my father returned from the funeral of his mother in Newcastle. Before he left, he'd asked us kids what we'd like him to bring back from the Big Smoke. 'A book', I said at once. I expected the latest Enid Blyton. What I got was *Moby Dick*. I was thrilled at the absence of pictures and the density of the print. A real book, and all mine.

It took me forever to read the first page of *Moby Dick*, and I didn't understand a thing. I knew what most of the words meant, but when they were assembled into sentences, they turned into a meaningless word salad. It would be another ten years before I could read it with a glimmer of understanding and actually enjoy Herman Melville's great work. Looking back, I should have considered myself fortunate in my father's choice of gift. He brought my mother a can of chocolate-coated ants. *Imported from Japan,* the label read. God knows what he and his brothers had been on at the wake prior to their gift-buying spree. The can sat in a kitchen cupboard for a few years before it disappeared.

I enjoyed *The Saint* book the most. The chapters consisted of self-contained short stories that I could generally finish in an hour or two. My initial impression in the library, that there was nothing 'racy' about the stories, was confirmed. However, Simon Templar, The Saint, inhabited a world that was as exotic and sophisticated as mine was claustrophobic and confined. He also possessed a personal quality that at the time I admired and wanted to emulate but couldn't put my finger on. When I moved to the city, my rural vocabulary expanded rapidly. At about the time that I acquired 'vibe', I also learned 'cool', destined to become and remain one of the overworked words of all time. The Saint was definitely Mr Cool. At fourteen, I understood the concept, even though I had yet to acquire the label.

The photos in the hunting book, *Lions to the Slaughter* (or whatever it was called), were compelling, but the prose that accompanied them was drab. The book was a boring read and I never finished it. *The Guns of Navarone* was all right, although I enjoyed the movie more, when I finally got to see it.

When I returned the books, the librarian gave me his thin smile. I wondered if it was a smile that he reserved just for me. I guess it must have been, as I never saw him smile at anybody else. Some time later an elderly man, even older that the librarian, came shuffling in to read the newspaper. He got a nod, but not a smile.

The librarian was dressed in the same shirt and tie he had worn the week before, although now there were what looked like food stains on his tie. Today he had removed his jacket, which hung on a wooden coat stand near the door.

'What did you think of the books?' he asked.

'Good', I replied. I felt I should elaborate, but couldn't think of anything to add.

The librarian opened his mouth as though he had something else to say, but let it go and deposited the books on the returned-book trolley.

The library was a cool, safe, place; a sanctuary. No traffic noises or raised voices penetrated the thick stone walls. The only sound was a faint hum from one of the fluorescent lights overhead and the rustling of paper as the old man turned the pages of the newspaper. Browsing the shelves, pulling down books and leafing through them, I had a delicious feeling of other-worldliness. Apart from the librarian and the old man at the end of the reading table, I had the place to myself.

I selected another volume in *The Saint* series and put it on the corner of a reading table under the watchful eye of the librarian. His eyes followed me everywhere. I could feel them even when my back was turned. It was more obvious than it had been on my first visit, but it was still creepy. Every time I caught his eye he looked back down at whatever he was doing on his desk. I don't know why, but it bothered me a bit because I couldn't see why he should be watching me. I wasn't about to stick a book under my jumper. In fact, I wasn't wearing a jumper. I guessed that he was interested in my choice of books. But he'd find that out soon enough when I checked them out.

Graduating to adult books was satisfying. I had a sense that I was going somewhere, but I wasn't sure where. I had left behind the books that had sustained me in my childhood, although I still got a guilty pleasure when I returned from time to time to *The Famous Five*—the adventures of Julian, Dick, Anne, George, and Timmy the dog, who inhabited a world that was a million miles from my own, a secret world I craved well into my early adolescence. A world of exotic things like picnic hampers, boarding schools, ruined castles, the seaside, sand and boats, islands with secret coves, bad men thwarted in their evil ways by four self-possessed children and their dog.

I chose two more books, as was my right. I can't remember what they were and I probably didn't finish them. I do remember the librarian turning them over in his hands and flipping through them, as he had done on my first visit, as though there was a secret somewhere in the pages. Again, the thin smile and the watery, crinkled eyes that held onto mine through thick horn-rimmed glasses. When I emerged from the library, blinking in the sunlight, it was like returning from some fantasy world to unwanted reality.

It was on my third visit that my relationship with the librarian suddenly changed. I had chosen yet another Leslie Charteris collection of short stories, along with a couple of other books, and was checking them out when he put a hand on my arm. It was the lightest of touch, but it made the hairs on my arm, such as they were, stand up. He picked up the collection of *Saint* stories, and said, 'You like these stories, it seems.'

'Yes', I replied, as I had the previous week. Feeling I should elaborate, I added, 'They're pretty good.'

'That's excellent', he said. 'But don't think you should be a little more, well, a little more adventurous?'

'Adventurous?' I looked at him uncertainly. He held my gaze for a moment with his pale eyes. I noticed they were rimmed with red. Then he looked down and removed his glasses to dab at his eyes with a handkerchief. Without his glasses, he looked like a different person.

He reached under his desk and produced a paperback book. There were hardly any paperbacks in the library. They were too easily destroyed, so libraries ordered hardback versions of books. If books were not available in hardback, they would buy paperbacks and turn them into hardbacks. This book, however, hadn't been re-covered. Also, I noticed, it was not a regular library book. It had no shelving code on the spine and carried no library stamp.

He must have noticed the look on my face, because he

said, 'It doesn't belong to the library; it's my own personal copy. Take care of it, but keep it as long as you like. I think you'll find it interesting.' He handed the book across the desk, using both hands as though it was something precious. It was a small book, a novel by the look of it. I dropped it into my bag, along with the other books, which he had stamped, and rode home.

I was dying to take a look at the book the librarian had lent me. What could be so special about a slim paperback? I shoved my bike into the back shed, entered the house, and headed for my bedroom. However, before I could even remove the books from my bag, my mother called out, reminding me that I had to accompany her to town.

It was that time, before the beginning of the new school year, when I had to take part in a humiliating rite: buying a new pair of school pants under my mother's supervision. I had to do this while the shop assistants, who had only been a couple of years ahead of me at school, sniggered in the background. I may have been given access to the adult library, but in my mother's eyes, I would, like Peter Pan, never grow up.

Buying clothes had become an annual event that took place when the clothing store held its back-to-school sale. When we were younger, our mother made all of our clothes. She was a brilliant seamstress and turned out wonderful shirts, shorts, and skirts, which were as embarrassing as hell to wear. They stamped us as different in a definitely un-cool way, and for children trembling on the edge of adolescence, there was no greater sin than to be different, as it invited exclusion at best and bullying at worst.

Having put up with the sniggers of my former class-mates, I returned home and rushed to my bedroom, eager to dip into the slim paperback the librarian was anxious for me to read.

The opening sentences hit me in a rush.

> If you really want to hear about it, the first thing you'll probably want to know is where I was born, and what my lousy childhood was like, and how my parents were occupied and all before they had me and all that David Copperfield kind of crap, but I don't feel like going into it if you want to know the truth. In the first place, that stuff bores me, and in the second place, my parents would have about two haemorrhages apiece if I told anything pretty personal about them. They're quite touchy about anything like that, especially my father. They're *nice* and all that— I'm not saying that—but they're also touchy as hell. Besides, I'm not going to tell you my whole goddam autobiography or anything. I'll just tell you about this madman stuff that happened to me around last Christmas just before I got pretty run-down and had to come out here and had to take it easy.

I'd never read anything like this before. It was as though the person behind the words was talking to me. And what he had to say about his parents rang like a gong in my head. My parents too were proud and private people, and my relationship with my father had started to fall apart. The previous night he had given me a lecture. I can't remember now what I'd done wrong; it was probably something minor like leaving his favourite spanner outside in the dirt after changing a tyre on my bike. In his eyes, that would be the equivalent of a major crime, as his tools were his pride and joy. When he caught you doing something wrong, you had to stand respectfully in front of him while he gave you a lecture. The lectures seemed to go on forever. Generally, he had little to say, but when he got wound up he could go on forever. I have no idea where the torrent of words came from—probably fuelled by half a dozen glasses of West End. When he ran out of new ideas, he repeated himself.

On one occasion, I got sick of it. My little brother was dancing around in the background, goading me into doing something stupid. It worked. I said, 'Hit me, Dad, don't shit me.' I was as amazed as my dad when I heard the words come out of my mouth. His face turned red and he lifted his arm. Instinctively, I cowered away, and raised my own arms to protect myself from what I knew was coming. He called it a box on the ears; I called it a punch in the head. He knocked me clean off my feet and said, 'Don't you ever shape up to me again, son.' The idea that I would shape up to my dad was laughable. He was pushing six feet tall and was an ex-prize fighter. I was pushing five foot six and couldn't fight my way out of a wet paper bag, as he had once noted. I went and lay on my bed and fantasised about all of the things I would do to him one day.

Physical abuse in the form of a punch in the head was euphemistically referred to as 'a box on the ears'. It may have happened more than once, but this is the only incident that sticks in my memory. It's the only time that I can remember a blow being delivered in hot blood. Usually, when we broke some aspect of our father's moral code (not difficult to do because it wasn't written down anywhere, and new rules seemed to be added at random: 'Don't pick your nose at the table!', 'Don't throw stones at the tethered goats on the hillside!'), he would lock us in the bathroom to 'think about what you've done'. We would sit quaking for what seemed like eternity on a three-legged wooden stool while our father went to have a beer and cool off. I generally thought not about the crime but about the punishment to come and how to get out of it. This usually involved blaming someone else ('Paul broke the branch off the tree') and never worked. Eventually came the dread sound of the door being unlocked and our father entering, leather belt in hand; the injunction to 'drop your pants'; the searing pain; the raised welts on buttocks and upper legs. This, appropriately, was known as a 'jolly-good belting'. If it was particularly severe, it was known as a 'jolly-good thrashing'.

Years later, my father is dead. I mention to my mother the time that my father knocked me to the ground in the heat of anger. She gives me a reproachful look and shakes her head. 'Your father adored you kids', she says. She may have been right, but at times, he sure had a funny way of showing it. It isn't until I have kids of my own that I understand; but by then he is long gone and it's far too late.

———

There was no mention of physical punishment being dished out to my new imaginary friend Holden Caulfield. His suffering was all mental, and self-inflicted.

That opening page of *The Catcher in the Rye* was my first encounter with a serious book—well, a library-type book— where the writer talked to me as though he had already taken a walk through my head. That night, I packed my collection of *Famous Five* books into a cardboard cartoon and pushed them under the bed.

I couldn't put the book down. What was it all about? The writer was holding back. I wanted to know what the 'madman stuff' was that happened just before Christmas, but he pulls me into the story without spilling the beans or even giving the slightest hint about what had happened. Instead he starts talking about his brother, to whom, presumably, he *did* spill the beans. He seemed to have a complicated relationship with his brother, who was a 'regular writer' of stories before prostituting himself to Hollywood. On the one hand, there was a sense of hero worship lurking behind the words. On the other hand, he disapproved of his brother becoming a screenwriter.

'I hate the movies', he tells me. 'Don't even mention them to me.' Well, how would I do that? He then says that he'll begin his story on the day he left Pencey Prep. 'You've probably heard of it', he says. Nope, sorry. I've never heard of it. I'm not even sure what a 'Prep.' is. It's obviously some kind of school. I guess that 'Prep' means 'preparatory', and that the school is preparing its inmates for something, but for what? Anyway, I've never heard of the school, even though he tells me that I probably have. From the Famous Five I learned that schools in other countries are very different from the one that had me entrapped. The Famous Five went to boarding school and they actually seemed to like it. I didn't mind school most of the time, but at three forty-five when the bell rang, I was on my bike and out of there.

The thing my friends who didn't read books (and that was most of them) didn't get was that they took you out of a place you didn't want to be and opened windows on worlds where strange things happened. Like kids going off to live in boarding school with all of their possessions in a thing called a 'trunk'. They went on picnics and ate sandwiches from a hamper. They had adventures. OK, so as a rapidly maturing adolescent, I was over all that and was ready for another fantasyland. The book that the librarian had placed in my hands offered the promise of an enticing new one.

I had yet to learn the name of the person who, in a couple of pages, had created an intimate relationship with me. His assessment of schools fitted in with mine. He described an advertisement that the school used to entrap parents. The text read: *Since 1888 we have been moulding boys into splendid, clear-thinking, young men.* His assessment of the advertisement was short and sweet:

> Strictly for the birds. They don't do any damn more *moulding* at Pencey than they do at any other school And I didn't know anybody there that was splendid and clear-thinking.

I couldn't agree more. There wasn't much moulding going on at my school. The teachers cared, and some of them tried hard, but the vast majority of the inmates couldn't see the point of what they were being forced to learn and looked on school as a meaningless ritual. So in fact there was nothing much for the teachers to mould.

I was about to find out what happened to him at Pencey Prep. on his last fateful day there when my mother knocked on the bedroom door. (Knocking—that was a new one. Maybe my dad had instructed her to do that so she wouldn't catch me doing something that would embarrass both of us.) Through the door, she called out that it was time for me to go to cricket practice. Cricket practice! Don't get me wrong (hmm, now I'm starting to sound like him), I loved playing cricket, and practice was OK, too, although I didn't much fancy facing up to Geoff Delbridge's deadly in-swingers on the concrete practice pitch. But right now I wanted to get on with the book.

———

On Monday morning, he was expecting me, that was clear. He accepted and processed my returned books before clearing his throat.

'So, what did you think?'

At that stage of my adolescence it was hard enough to figure out what my feelings were, much less put them into words. I ignored his question, and asked one of my own.

'Why did you give me this?'

'I could tell right away how smart you are', he replied, 'and I didn't want you to waste your whole summer on that rubbish you were borrowing.'

'I don't think they're rubbish', I wanted to say, but kept my mouth shut. It's true that the book he had pressed on me was profoundly different from, and infinitely superior to, anything I had ever read, but that didn't mean that *The Saint* and other stories were rubbish. Anyway, I didn't want to start an argument that I knew I couldn't possibly win.

'And there is one other thing', he said.

'What's that?'

'Holden Caulfield reminded me of you. And I thought that you might see yourself in him.'

Again, there was so much I wanted to say, and again, I kept my mouth shut. Holden's views on many things made sense to me, that was true; but he came from such a different world, and there was something seriously wrong with his head. Was that how the librarian saw me—as a completely cuckoo kid?

All these years later, writing about what happened back then, I'm pursued by a question as I try to bring those long dead incidents back to life. What was really going on in my head at the time? My memory of the physical facts of the matter are clear and vivid. I'm certain of the green linoleum floor, the thick stone walls, and the smell of beeswax and book dust that hit me every time I entered the library. I remember clearly the way that the librarian's red-rimmed eyes followed me about. But I'm not at all sure about what was going on in my head.

I'm not a rebellious type. Never have been. By nature, I'm not confrontational, which has sometimes got me into serious trouble. There are times when dealing with conflict head-on leads to a split lip, but it can also resolve the conflict. As a general rule, I clung to the belief that if you ignored a problem, it would go away. But of course it rarely did. Problems and conflicts could never be wished away.

Some people seem to sail through life without conflict. Others are never out of trouble and strife. Why do some kids rebel? Why do some never feel the need? Maybe for some, rebellion is unnecessary.

Holden Caulfield and I could not have been more different, but when I thought about it I realised that the librarian had got it right in one sense. We were both non-confrontational and liked to fight out battles in our head. In that particular regard, we could both be quite heroic. Like Holden, I won most of the fights that I had with myself.

The librarian rifled through the little paperback. Then he found the page he was looking for. 'This is what the book is all about', he said, and ran his thumb down the paragraph.

> I'm standing on the edge of some crazy cliff. What I have to do, I have to catch everybody if they start to go over the cliff—I mean if they're running and they don't look where they're going I have to come out from somewhere and catch them. That's all I'd do all day. I'd just be the catcher in the rye and all.

And then, out of the blue, he looked up from the book and invited me to his house. Again, I remember the incident itself as though it were yesterday. However, I don't remember what I thought or what I felt way back then when the invitation came.

The conversation went something like this:

'Library's closing. I have to lock up soon.'

'All right.' I felt as though I should say more, make some witty or intelligent observation about the book, but nothing came to mind. I didn't even thank him for the considerable favour he had done in lending me the book.

'I've got some other books at home that you might like', he says. 'Why don't you come back to my place? Have a cold drink. You can look at the books and see if there's anything you fancy. It's a private collection. Volumes you wouldn't find in the library.'

'I have to go to cricket practice.'

'Cricket?' It's clear from his expression that I've fallen well below his expectations. 'Perhaps tomorrow, then?'

He gave me the address and said he'd be there after five.

———

I nearly didn't go, but I was curious. So, shortly after five o'clock the following day, I push my bike up the little laneway behind William Street just north of the town centre.

It's an old stone house, one of the very few stone houses in the town, and is perched on a slight rise, providing its inhabitants with a view over the dusty central shopping area. It looks quite solid. It has a patch of lawn struggling to survive out the front and some rose bushes at the side.

The door is opened by a boy about my own age. I look at him in surprise. He looks back at me without emotion. He has a head of soft black curls and his skin is very pale. 'Come in', he says in a low voice. He has an accent of some kind, but I have no idea what it is. Certainly not a foreign accent—not like the Greeks, the Italians, and the Yugoslavs —but different from mine. He turns and I follow him down the hall.

The librarian is sitting in a lounge chair, legs crossed, listening to music. He gives me that thin smile of his and uncrosses his legs, although he doesn't stand up.

'I'm so pleased that you could come', he says. Then, 'Call me Henny.'

I could never do that. I don't call him anything.

Music comes grinding out of an old gramophone player. I've never seen one like it. It sits on a table in a brown Bakelite case and has a crooked arm that holds the needle. The needle and arm go up and down as the disk goes round and round. Someone is singing in a high, thin voice. It doesn't sound English, although it's hard to tell. The record is very cracked, and the player makes a hissing noise.

'It's Mahler', he says.

I've never head of a singer called Mahler. I don't think

much of it. We are on the edge of the pop revolution, and this kind of stuff that the librarian fancies makes even old crooners like Frank Sinatra and Tony Bennett sound modern.

'Would you like a drink?' He does the uncrossing and crossing of his leg thing again. Jiggles his foot. If I didn't know better, I'd say he was nervous.

'Yeah. Thanks.'

'What would you like?'

'Coke.' Pause. 'Thanks.'

'I don't have Coke. I have tonic water, or bitter lemon.'

'Bitter lemon. Thanks.'

He turns his head and speaks to the boy who is lurking by the door.

'Kevin, a bitter lemon with ice; and can you bring me my glass?' Then, as an afterthought: 'And you can get a drink for yourself if you want one.'

The boy disappears.

'Is he your son?' I ask. This is the first time I've initiated a conversation. It's the first time I've said more than a word or two. They look nothing like each other, and the librarian looks far too old to have children, but you just never know about these things. He laughs. 'No, he's not my son. He's a friend. He's staying with me.'

I don't know what to say. In my limited universe, old men didn't have male friends a fraction of their age, but what would I know? I'm beginning to realise that the world is a mysterious and unexpected place. I wonder if that's how he thinks of me—as a friend.

Kevin comes back into the room. He hands me the glass of bitter lemon, and gives the librarian a glass. The glass is elegant, with a long thin stem. The librarian takes the stem between thumb and forefinger and goes to the sideboard. He pours himself something dark and sticky-looking from a bottle on the sideboard. Then he returns to his seat, a straight-backed chair set in a corner of the room. Stares at me blankly. Says nothing. In his own home it seems that he doesn't feel the need to pretend that he isn't looking at me.

When I was younger, I remember seeing glasses like that in my grandfather's house. My grandfather was long dead, and the house was inhabited by an uncle and aunt. The glasses were left over from the days when our grandfather amounted to something around town, and one by one they got broken. The glasses in our house used to contain Vegemite and peanut paste and other spreadable sandwich fillings. When they were empty, mum would soak off their labels and they would become glasses. No-one cared much if they got broken.

We sit in silence for a while, and then he starts giving me a lecture. I'm looking at the old piano in the corner. I don't really know what he's talking about. I feel uncomfortable. I thought the idea was for me to come here and look at books...

'Only English poetry', he says. 'Or Irish—the only thing they're good for. The English for all types of literature, of course. The Dutch for art. Germans for music. And the French ... The French.' He sighs. I know what he's up to. He's showing me how smart he is. He's knowledgeable, clearly, but then he's a librarian. He has nothing to do all day except sit in that cool, dim room and acquire knowledge. That, and stamping the occasional book.

He settles his glass carefully on a side table, then strolls across the room and removes a book from the large bookcase beside the piano. It has thick speckled pages and a brown leather cover. 'What poets do you know?'

I shrug. 'Not that many. We did Banjo Patterson in school. He was all right. And Henry Lawson.'

'Minor figures', he says. 'No-one will remember them in 100 years.'

All this time, Kevin stares at us, his hands tucked under his thighs. He has a bruised and troubled look. I wonder where he came from and what he's doing here, but ask for no explanation and none is given. He seems a very odd friend for the librarian to have.

The librarian thumbs through the pages of the book, scans a page, and then hands the book to me. 'Read this', he says.

I begin reading the poem to myself.

'Out loud', he says.

I stumble through the poem. Some of the words I understand; many of them I don't. Overall, the poem is utterly incomprehensible.

'Well', says the librarian as I limp through the last stanza, 'At least you can read. Not like poor Kevin over there. I've tried to help him, but it's a lost cause.'

I'm totally confused. Why would the librarian, whose existence appears to revolve around books, choose some strange, illiterate kid to be his companion? He retrieves the book, claps it shut, and hands it to me.

'Why don't you borrow it? I think you're just about ready for poetry. Real poetry. Find one you like and practice it. You can read it to me next week. Same time.'

Not a word about whether I might want to come back next week. He just assumes that I'll be dying to get back to continue my education. At last he's found a lump of clay he can mould. Anyway, it's clear that this visit is over. I leave the unfinished glass of bitter lemon on the armrest of the lounge, and he shows me to the door.

Relieved, I jump on my bike and ride away, easier now as it's downhill. There will be no second visit. There is something scary about the house. The cool dim space inside was similar to the library, except that there was something different in the air. I couldn't say what it was, but walking into the house was stepping into a different world. It's a world I don't know, and it's one that I don't want to know. It's good to be back in the bright world, boring as it is, with the sun on my back as I pedal home.

Next day, I see a problem in the form of a book of poems sitting on the edge of the little deal desk in my room. In my haste to get away, I had taken the book with me. Hadn't even thought about it. These days, libraries and video shops have an 'after hours' return slot where borrowed items can be conveniently returned without the need for human contact. But not back then.

My first thought, coward that I am, is to have someone else return it for me. But no-one else comes to mind. Most of my friends, even my cousins, are away for the Christmas holiday. It seems such a trivial problem these days, but it wasn't back then.

I leave it for two days, and then, late in the afternoon, return the books to the library. He looks up when I enter the room. 'I thought you had forgotten,' he says. He gives me that scary smile.

'I need to give you this.' I hand over the book of poetry. I'm nervous. He's in full control, and he knows that I know. When I first met him I thought he was a harmless old man;

a pervert, perhaps, but harmless. Now, I'm not so sure. There's something dark about him.

'Oh', he says. 'Don't worry about it. Keep it. When you come on Friday, I have some other books to show you. Different books.'

Friday? Had I agreed to go back to his house on Friday? Different books? What was he talking about?

I should have dropped the book on his desk and walked out of the library for good. Instead, I find myself riding slowly home, the book still in my possession. When I get home, I put it back on the corner of my desk and go down to the cricket nets on the corner of Hillside Oval to be terrorised by Geoff Delbridge with his deadly, late in-swingers. This kind of terrorizing I can deal with. This kind I'm familiar with. As to Friday, I have four days to decide what to do. For the moment I put the librarian, his house, and his books out of my mind.

The week passes slowly. Because he works Saturdays, Dad has Friday off. My brother is quick enough to disappear somewhere into the neighbourhood while our Dad is still eating his bacon, eggs, and toast. He catches me lounging on my bed reading a book. Had it been a book designed to improve my mind, I might have got away with it, but it's a novel. These are not designed to improve the mind—or anything else, for that matter. They are harmless (or not-so-harmless) forms of entertainment. In other words, they are mindless, only to be turned to in the evening when the day's work is done. Dad uses novels as a sleeping aid. It takes him forever to get through a slim paperback, as he has to read on the succeeding evening the pages he had read on the previous night. Eventually, he will be saved by the arrival of television. He considers most of the programs, particularly British comedies, rubbish, but he watches them anyway.

I'm hauled off the bed and marched into the backyard. Dad has an inexhaustible fund of proverbs and aphorisms, most of which I find either incomprehensible or just plain stupid. One of his favourites is, 'Cleanliness is next to Godliness.' What on earth does it mean? That salvation comes in the form of a cake of green Palmolive soap? In school we were taught that God was flanked on one side by his Son and on the other by the Holy Ghost, with St. Peter in the wings. There was never any mention of a cake of soap.

This morning, he mutters, 'The devil finds work for idle hands.'

Does this make you the devil, Dad? I'm tempted to ask, but keep my mouth shut for once. I find it interesting that an avowed atheist's life is guided by religious clichés.

I'm directed into the hen house, or chook shed, to shovel dried sheets of chicken shit into a wheelbarrow, to be subsequently forked around Mum's struggling roses. Then I'm handed a pitchfork and instructed to turn over a patch of earth. In time, this will also receive its quota of chicken shit, ready to be planted out with vegetable seedlings.

While I struggle with chicken shit and rich, red earth, Dad alternates between fixing me with a watchful eye and mixing a batch of concrete by hand. Dad belongs to a generation that believes in the virtue of concrete. This is about as close as he comes to religion. He sees no virtue whatsoever in bare earth. If you can't grow something on it, then you concrete it over. When he says, 'I'm just going to tidy over that bit of the yard', we know he means that he's going to eclipse it with a slab of concrete.

It's just my luck that on this particular Friday, summer has returned with a vengeance. By mid-morning my face is fiery red; by lunchtime I'm exhausted. Dad, on the other hand, works steadily away, seemingly unaffected by the blazing sun. He wears an old straw hat, a blue workman's singlet, shorts, and a pair of steel-capped boots, passed on to him by one of his mates from the mine.

Over lunch (lettuce and tomato salad covered in home-made mayonnaise, and slices of pickled ox tongue), he gives me my tasks for the afternoon. However, I have other ideas. As the morning progresses, the cool, dim reaches of the librarian's living room and a glass of bitter lemon and ice become increasingly attractive.

After lunch, I put in another hour turning soil and shifting shit in the old wheelbarrow with the squeaky metal wheel. Dad is mixing and carting concrete in a fancier, newer wheelbarrow with a pneumatic wheel. Years ago he had announced that mixing cement by hand was a mug's game. Uncle Jimmy had bought himself an electric mixer because he was building himself a house and there was no way that he was going to mix the cement for thousands of house bricks by hand.

From then on, whenever Dad needed to do any cementing (which was surprisingly frequently) he borrowed the electric mixer. However, on this particular day Jimmy had lent the mixer to a mate, and so Dad had to revert to the traditional practice of mixing concrete in a wheelbar-row. If he'd had the patience to wait until Sunday, he could have avoided the backbreaking work of mixing the concrete by hand, but that was not Dad's way.

It's touch and go when I put lean my pitchfork against the side of the chook shed and make it clear that I'm done for the day. Things can go either way. There are times when he's thankful—grateful even—for my help. Other times, he makes it clear that I have a duty to 'Pull my weight.'

Dad looks up from floating off the slab of concrete. 'Tossing in the towel, are you?'

'I have to go to the library. Have to return a book. I forgot. I'll come back later.'

'Forget it', he says, and turns his back. His concrete is drying out faster than he wants. If it dries too quickly, it will crack. He has to finish floating it off, take a break, and then spray it with water so that the surface doesn't dry too quickly. The sun has taken its toll, and it's clear that he's begun to think of a cleansing ale.

The bottles of beer stand like soldiers at the back of the fridge. Twenty-six-ounce bottles, never stubbies. A mere degree or two above freezing. Dad is a beer aficionado. When he goes drinking, he carries a thermometer in the top pocket of his jacket. Occasionally, he whips this out to test the temperature of the beer that is pulled from the tap. If it's over 35 degrees, there's bound to be trouble. The only publican he really trusts is Mario. When he drinks at Mario's, the thermometer never comes out of his pocket.

———

I expect Kevin to open the door, but it's the librarian himself. He peers around the half open door at me as though expecting someone else. When he sees it's me, he gives me that half-smile. Although his eyes crinkle, his smile stops at his nose. He steps aside and says, 'Come in, come in. I wasn't sure that you'd turn up.'

He leads me down the corridor to the lounge room. It's

exactly the same as on my previous visit—curtains drawn to keep out the heat and most of the light, heavy furniture, doilies on the occasional tables. The sort of place you'd expect might belong to an old lady. I put the book of poetry on the dining table, and hope that he doesn't give me a quiz.

'Where's Kevin?' I ask, looking around.

'Ah', he says, with a faint air of regret, 'Kevin doesn't live here any more.'

For some reason, I find this information unsettling. 'Where... where did he go?'

He ignores my question, offers me a seat—the same armchair I had sat in last time—and crosses to the table that holds his collection of records and the turntable. He selects a record, extracts it carefully from its sleeve, and puts it onto the turntable. The music is mournful—the kind you might expect to hear at a funeral. At that stage, I had only ever been to one funeral, that of my friend Billy, who'd been knocked down by a hit-run driver as he rode his bike home from school. They played this kind of music at his funeral, although there was no singing, not like on the librarian's record.

'Monteverdi', he says. 'What do you think?'

I make a noise that I hope sounds appreciative and nod my head.

'Very different from the Mahler that I played for you the other day, eh?'

To be honest, they sound the same to me, but I duck my head again.

He gives me a little lecture on Monteverdi. 'Much older than Mahler, of course, as you can tell from the music. Three hundred years older, in fact. Hard to believe now, but in his day he was considered dangerously radical. Many people consider him to be the father of the Baroque period. He could also be considered the father of opera.'

I sit there nodding my head like a clown in a sideshow. I wonder where this conversation is going. The answer is nowhere.

'Drink?' he asks.

'Ta!' I know that in polite company I'm supposed to say 'Yes, please', as my mother has taught me, but the lecture on Monteverdi has caught me off guard. Anyway, I'm not sure whether the librarian constitutes polite company.

'I have Coca-Cola', he says smugly. 'I remember that's what you asked for last time.'

'Ta!' I say again. He disappears into the kitchen and returns a short time later carrying a tray containing a small bottle of Coke with the cap removed, a tumbler, and two of the elegant wine glasses. He fills the tumbler and sets it on an occasional table at my knee. Then he crosses to the sideboard and fills one of the wine glasses from a decanter. Then he turns to me, pauses, and asks if I would like to try some. He acts as thought he's just thought of this, but he must have had it in mind because he brought out two wine glasses.

'What is it?' I ask.

'Marsala wine. It's slightly alcoholic, but not too bad.'

'All right, just a bit.' I don't really want it but don't know how to refuse politely.

He half-fills the second glass and hands it to me. It looks sweet and sickly, and that's exactly how it tastes.

To this point, my experiences with alcohol have been strictly limited. Some years ago, my brother Paul and I raided the sideboard in the lounge room late one afternoon when we were bored and our parents were at the pub. We helped ourselves to Dad's collection of sample bottles of alcohol, given to him as a gift by one of the traveling salesman who used to knock on the front door from time to time. We consumed the sweet sherry and the White Heather Whisky. While Paul was being sick, I replaced the contents of the little bottles with apple cordial from the fridge. Our Dad only drank beer in those days, and so our crime was safe until the whiskey priest came to visit our mother and was offered a snifter from one of the sample bottles. It was highly embarrassing for Mum and extremely painful for us. It also put Paul off alcohol for most of his succeeding adolescence, although he made up for it in later years.

'Won't you come and sit over here?' says the librarian, patting the sofa cushion next to him.

'I'm fine here', I say.

'It would be better over here', says the librarian, sounding slightly irritated. 'I have some books I want to show you. They're art books.'

Somewhat reluctantly, I move over to the sofa. The librarian disappears into one of the front rooms, which I presume is a bedroom, and reappears a short time later carrying a couple of large hardcover books. He puts one of these on the coffee table and sits down beside me on the sofa with the other one on his knees. The cover of the book is protected by a heavy plastic dust jacket. It features a large photograph of a classical marble statue. The statue is of a young man, stark naked, staring dreamily off into the distance.

'Have you seen this before?' asks the librarian.

'I'm not sure', I reply.

'You're not sure? Surely you've either seen it or you haven't.'

'Well, I've seen pictures of old statues before, but I'm not sure whether I've seen that one or not.'

'If you've seen this one before you should remember it. It's one of the greatest sculptures of all time. Michelangelo's *David*.' He announces the name of the statue with a reverential air, and traces the outline of the statue's forefinger. 'Such beauty! What do you think?'

He has this habit of asking me for my opinion. *What do I think of this novel? What do I think of that book of poems? What do I think of the music? What do I think of the wine?* The questions make me uncomfortable. I don't feel old enough or qualified enough to have an opinion about anything much, apart from the quality of our local football team and the shapeliness of our neighbour Bonnie's breasts. To be honest, the statue looks like any of those other ancient statues that you sometimes see in library books. So I do my usual trick of saying nothing and seeking salvation in a nod of the head.

He turns the pages slowly, lovingly. The book consists mainly of photographs, with a bit of text here and there. The photographs show statues or paintings of young males in various poses and various stages of nakedness. One painting shows a figure with his hands tied behind his back. Soldiers are shooting arrows into him. From the look on his face, however, he doesn't seem to be feeling much pain. He just has a faint look of regret, as though he has lost something.

The librarian finally puts the book aside and picks up the other one from the coffee table.

'This is a very special book', he said. 'You won't find it in the bookshops.' He begins leafing through the pages, looking closely at the images as though seeing them for the first time. These paintings are all modern, but they're about the same subject as the first book: They all show images of boys or young men. After turning over a few pages, he hands the book to me. 'Beautiful, aren't they?' he says. 'You can take a look. There's nothing wrong, you know. This is art.' Then he stands up and moves to the sideboard with our wine glasses. 'I'll get us another drink.'

'So', he says, returning with the glasses and setting them on the little table. 'What do you think?'

I have no idea what to think. I don't know what to say. Why is he showing me this stuff? Finally, I say, 'They're nice.'

'Nice? Is that what you think? What I think is that we have to work on your art appreciation.' He gives my knee a friendly squeeze. 'Let's pick one and talk about it.' He relieves me of the book and flips through the pages, then stops and points to a picture. 'Let's discuss this one.'

'This one' is a simple black-and-white line drawing showing the reclining figure of a young boy against a grey background, which looks to be a watercolour wash. The boy has his arms stretched out behind him. His eyes are closed, and he appears to be sleeping. He has curly hair and full lips. He seems to be lying on a bed, with his legs dangling over the end. He is naked apart for a pair of shorts, one leg of which is gaping open, revealing his penis. It's fairly indistinct, because the shading around his groin is darker than other parts of his body, but it's clearly a penis. It looks, well, wrong. Not from a sexual point of view—that kind of thing doesn't bother me. It just seems kind of corny. Embarrassing. Laughable almost. What was the artist trying to prove?

'It's the simplicity, you see', says the Librarian, running his finger across the boy's torso. He seems to like touching the reproductions. 'It's a Friend.'

I look at him amazed. This young boy—well, he can't be that young, he has a smudge of hair in his armpit. This boy is a friend of his? 'You know him?'

He looks at me, puzzled for a moment, and then laughs. 'Oh, no', he says. 'It's painted by Donald Friend. He's an artist. I don't suppose you've ever heard of him.'

'Nope.' I'm beginning to get used to my ignorance, and it doesn't bother me now, not like it did when I first began having conversations with the librarian. He snaps the book shut and mutters something about ignorance and bliss.

'Would you like to borrow this one? You'd have to be careful with it; it's quite valuable.'

'Oh, no, it's all right', I say. I have nowhere at home to hide such a large book.

He puts the book carefully on the table next to his glass and turns to me. The skin under his neck wobbles. He is wearing the dark green tie that is spotted with food. He leans towards me. I open my mouth to say I have to go when he kisses me full on the mouth. His breath is hot and sweet, his lips fat and wet. I pull away.

'I think we should have a cuddle', he says. He starts fiddling with his pants. Unbuckled, his pants drop to his knees. I stare, mesmerised, horrified as he fishes his penis from his underpants. He has the same kind of underwear as my Dad— boxers that come almost to his knobby knees. Desperately unfashionable undergarments that cover the body from navel to knee. His penis is flaccid, mottled, and flops along his thigh. He plays with it and it starts to move in his hand. I stare at it, horrified but fascinated at the same time. By that stage I was having erections of my own—pretty constantly, actually—but this is the first time that I have seen a fully fledged adult penis in action.

I have no script for what should happen next. I sit there, frozen, as his penis grows, still soft in his hand, but immense. The spell is broken when he reaches across, grabs my wrist, and begins to steer my hand towards his upper thigh. I wrench my hand away, jump to my feet, and back away. He tries to come after me, but his pants—around his ankles now—make progress impossible unless he hops towards me like a kangaroo. They trip him up and he falls on his face. I head for the door.

———

Back then, homosexuality was even more mysterious than regular sex. Those infected with the disease were known as 'homos' or 'poofs' or, among more genteel adults, as 'One of Those', as in, 'I think that Mavis's second boy is One of Those.' In the 1960s, the word 'gay' had connotations other than homosexuality. We knew that homosexuals existed, that they were among us, but they were invisible, like aliens from outer space, Masons, or the Mormons.

THE GIRL WITH THE GOLDEN PLAIT

I guess I shouldn't have blamed Robbie. After all, it was because of him that I got to look at her the way I did. It happened towards the end of yet another long, hot summer holiday. Robbie came back from visiting his grandparents in Adelaide and brought with a magazine along with a lot of other stuff. It was a catalogue from a sports store, and had coloured illustrations of swim fins, sports bikes, and inflatable swimming pools that you put on the back lawn in summer, if you had a back lawn, where they collected neighbours' leaves and bred mosquitoes. That sort of thing.

'Look at these', Robbie said. 'Skateboards. They're the latest thing.'

'Wow!' I was impressed. I was also a little surprised that he hadn't brought one back from the city with him. As the only child of the only family in the neighbourhood with money, he specialised in latest things.

'They were all sold out', he said. 'But Granp ordered one. He'll bring it when he and Gran come up for Easter.'

Easter was way off on the horizon, so in the interim we

decided to make our own skateboard. We disassembled the pair of skates Robbie had been given for Christmas, retained the wheel assembly, and threw the base and straps away. Then we pulled a wooden paling from the McCartney's back fence, crafted it with a fretsaw into something approximating the shape of the skateboard in the sports catalogue, and screwed on the wheels from the skates.

The only place smooth enough to road-test our makeshift board was the concrete stormwater drain that bisected our neighbourhood. As it only rained once in a blue moon, the drain had few practical uses. Smoking under the Wills Street bridge was one of them. Maybe skateboarding would be another.

From the roadside, the curve of the drain looked daunting.

'You go first', said Robbie.

'You. It's your board.'

'It's ours. I'm the engineer. You're the test pilot. You go first.'

'You go first.

This went on for while as we stared down into the drain. Inevitably, I went first. Robbie always got his way.

I balanced the board on the edge of the culvert and stood on it. It wobbled from side to side, and I almost fell off before I'd begun. I got some curious looks from shoppers coming and going at the Service Stores across the street. I was about to rethink the whole venture when Robbie gave me a shove, and I sailed off into the stormwater drain. Gravity kept me upright to the bottom and halfway up the other side. It then pulled me backwards and dumped me face down on the concrete. On descent, the skateboard, which had flipped into the air, hit me on the back of the head. I rolled over and freed my two front teeth from the flesh of my upper lip. Blood was running down the back of my throat. I spat it out and opened my eyes. Then I felt into my mouth and was relieved that my teeth were still intact.

Robbie hadn't moved. He just stood there looking down at the skateboard, which had broken in two when it hit me on the head. Standing a little apart from Robbie was the girl. She was looking down at me with a slightly puzzled look, as though she'd just witnessed a circus trick that had gone badly wrong. I looked up at a pair of long brown legs that ended in a pair of tight crimson shorts. From where I lay, I could see a flash of white below the shorts before she turned and walked away. A single thick blonde plait bounced from side to side as she walked. Robbie watched her go and then scrambled down into the drain.

'Jeez', he said. 'Did you see that? Did you see those legs? Where did she come from?'

I fussed at my lip and felt the lump on the back of my head. Robbie inspected the busted skateboard and chucked it away under the road bridge.

———

The final week of the holidays limped by. I endured the embarrassing ritual of having to shop with my mother for school clothes. This was my annual exercise in parental humiliation, and as I moved through adolescence, the humiliation only got worse. At The Corner Haberdashery, two young shop assistants, former classmates, stood smirking in the background as my mother rifled through the 'back to school specials' basket. I grudgingly agreed to a pair of short pants of a most unfashionable cut, but drew the line at a 'sensible' sun hat. There was just so much humiliation I could take. No-one wore sun hats. Sunstroke was more the thing.

I laboured through pre-school chores: ruled up my exercise books, and wrote 'JMJ' at the top of each page. This was to remind us that our academic labours were for the love we held in our hearts for Jesus, Mary, and Joseph. I put new second-hand tyres on my second-hand bike and oiled the chain, envying Robbie his new three-speed bike—another Christmas gift. Like all of his possessions, it was The Latest Thing; a Skid Kid, and a geared one at that. And all week, at the back of my mind was the girl with the golden plait. I roamed the neighbourhood in hopes of catching a glimpse of her, but the expeditions were as successful as the *Search for the Golden Boomerang*, a radio serial that I was rapidly outgrowing.

The drudgery of the new school year. The teachers are no more enthusiastic than the kids; and several have, over the Christmas break, discovered some interesting new ways of displaying their grumpiness. A late season heat wave does nothing for anyone's enthusiasm, and a general air of listlessness hangs over the school. Otherwise thing are pretty much the same as they were in December. Guido Delabosca is alternately pilloried and shunned for stinking of garlic. Skinny Atkin and his gang of thugs terrorise the school yard. And Fatty Harvey has thumb tacks spread on his seat: punishment for his fat bum.

The focus of my attention in that first week is avoiding being drafted into the school choir. All of the boys in the junior school are hauled out of class in batches and consigned to the school hall. Here we're made to stand shoulder to shoulder and sing *Over the Sea to Skye* while Brother Leo, the choirmaster, creeps along behind us, eavesdropping on our performance. This is the third year in a row that I've been auditioned, and I'm confident that I can once again avoid the draft. Most of the kids in my class have already gone through or are in the throes of puberty, and their voices soar from baritone to tenor at the drop of a hat. They're instantly rejected. Although I went through puberty at the extraordinarily early age of eleven, my voice has not broken. My balls descended, but my voice didn't follow. Despite this, singing out of tune is a piece of cake. I'm therefore shocked to the core when Brother Leo taps me on the shoulder and points in the direction of the glum-looking knot of boys sulking at the far end of the hall. I'm officially designated a loser. We are told to return to the hall after school for an initial rehearsal.

'Bad luck', says Robbie, and laughs, as we trudge back to class. Although he had managed to avoid the draft, he's in a bad mood because some envious little shit had scratched the frame of his new Skid Kid. Well, what did you expect? Many of the kids in the school couldn't even afford a broken-down second-hand bike, let alone a new one. Silence. And then: 'I think I saw her.'

I look at him.

'The leggy sheila', he says. 'The one with the plait.'

I was surprised that she was as much on his mind as she was on mine. Robbie didn't work like that. He skated effort-lessly on the surface of life. As a teacher once said to him, 'Robbie, you have a mind of unfathomable shallows.'

I say nothing. I have a lump in my throat. And I'm still pissed off at being drafted into the choir.

'You remember her?'

'Kinda', I reply, as casually as I can.

'She's something else. Those legs. I think about them all the time. Wonder where she came from? How come we never see her around town?'

'Who knows?'

We enter the classroom. Brother Viator, also known as 'Piggy', tells us to shut up and get to our seats.

————

Shortly after Robbie was born, his mother was diagnosed with a serious heart condition. It was a congenital condition that only revealed itself under the strain of pregnancy and labour. During Robbie's childhood it got worse. By the time he was ten, his mother was an invalid. She and my mother were friends. They were both gentle, decent women who mostly kept to themselves and maintained minimal contact with the miners' wives who made up most of the neighbourhood.

Because of the friendship between our mothers, I called Robbie's mother 'Aunty Marg', even though she was no relation. The interests of consistency demanded that I call his father 'Uncle Henry'. Judging by the wedding photos that stood on a table in the hallway, Aunty Marg had been a great beauty. One day I overheard my father wondering out loud to my mother what had possessed her to throw herself away on Henry Roebuck. I remember her as a fragile woman sitting patiently on the back verandah, a cotton blanket over her knee. She would sit there for hours, staring at Tammy, Robbie's pet lamb. Tammy disappeared one day and turned up on the dining table, much to Robbie's distress and his father's amusement.

Aunty Marg's condition got worse. The doctors decided that open-heart surgery was the only option. These days, such procedures are pretty standard. In the 1960s they were high risk. The family conferred and agreed with the doctors —well, in those days you just did. There was no such thing as a second opinion. She took the train to Melbourne for the operation. Uncle Henry couldn't go with her; he had to stay at home and tend to his business. We all went to the station to see her off. 'See you in a few weeks', everyone all cried cheerfully. 'The Big Smoke, eh? Lucky thing!' and 'Watch out for those Melbourne men.' It was the only time in my life that I ever saw Robbie cry.

When I get home from school, Mum takes me into her bedroom and closes the door. She makes me sit on the bed, and stands in front of me. She has started to develop a double chin, and it quivers slightly as she speaks. 'Aunty Marg didn't make it', she says. 'The operation was just too much for her.' My mother doesn't cry. She rarely cried. Just occasionally. Like when she had to give us a beating—tears would run down her cheek as she whacked us with a leather strap or length of deal.

'Go and see Robbie', she says.

'I will.'

I climb the hill at the end of the street and sit there for a long time looking at the corrugated iron roofs and dusty eucalypts. Robbie disappears from school for two weeks and then reappears as though nothing had happened. He is as outgoing as ever, accepts our shuffling condolences —'Sorry, mate! Bad luck'—and slots back into school life. But there is something different in the way he talks. His voice has completely broken.

Uncle Henry had a second-hand car lot on the edge of

the city block. This allowed him to call himself a businessman and gave him access to the Broken Hill Club, a refuge from unionists and other riff-raff, where mine managers and shop owners could drink whisky. He was affable, running to fat, and had thinning hair that he treated with California Poppy and a comb-over. He also had a crude streak. He liked to tell fart jokes, which he thought were hilarious. He had a fart cushion, (bought from a mail order catalogue, where it was called a 'whoopie cushion') that he would place on the chair of unsuspecting guests. Still, he was kind enough, and dealt with the tragic death of his beautiful wife by spoiling Robbie rotten. Robbie accepted the endless stream of gifts and games as a natural part of life. They piled up, often unopened, in the spare room that I guess had once been intended for a younger brother. Those of us who got to see his store of treasures were as envious as hell.

———

And then, one day, I have a sighting. I'm messing about on my bike in the vacant block next to my aunt's house when, sensing a presence, I look up—and there she is. She's standing under a tall ghost gum on the opposite side of the street observing me. Inspecting me! I smile at her, but I guess it comes out as a lopsided leer. She drops her head, turns, and walks into the house that sits behind the gum tree. As she moves, her haunches sway from side to side like a young animal that carries the bulk of its weight in the rear. The screen door clatters shut and she is gone.

The last time I noticed the house across the street it had been inhabited by a grumpy old bag called Mrs Gough.

When we were young, my cousin Pete and I threw gravel on her roof. Suddenly she appeared on the verandah and shook her stick at us. Convinced she was a witch and scared shit-less, we ran all the way up the lane, around the corner store, and into the safety of Pete's bedroom.

Gravel on a corrugated iron roof sounds like a short, sharp shower of rain. A lump of rock sounds like the start of World War III. As adolescents, our preferred method of getting our mates out at night was to lob a handful of gravel (or, if we disliked their parents, a brick) onto their roof. Occasionally a parent would rush out in fury and shout into the night, but more usually the intended recipient of the message would appear from the shadows and we would go marauding. Nothing too serious, mind you—just innocent stuff like minor theft and vandalism.

I ask my aunt about the newcomers across the street. Mrs Gough died in her sleep (as she lived alone, how anyone would know this, I have no idea) and, being without family, her house was sold as a deceased estate. The place is bought by the Khitrovos, a family of White Russians. The reference to White Russians puzzles me. The girl with the golden plait has creamy brown-coloured skin. I wonder whether the Russian race is divided into blacks and whites, like the Americans. Or maybe it has to do with hair colour-ing. However, that doesn't make much sense to me either. At school, I have a Yugoslavian friend called Tony who comes from a family of blondes. However, no-one calls them the White Yugoslavs. It's only later, when they teach us about the evils of communism, that I learn about the Reds and make the connection. Russia is an impossibly remote and mysterious place. The only connection to our world are the sputniks that glide silently over the night sky and the Bay of Pigs fiasco that had our parents and teachers convinced the end of the world was only a week away.

My aunt tells me that the Khitrovos are a nice family. They are quiet and keep to themselves. The family consists of an elderly grandfather, parents, and two children—a boy (well, a young man, really) and a younger girl.

'Very pretty', says my aunt.

'Oh, really?' I reply.

'She's the only one who speaks a bit of English. So they send her out to do the shopping. I see her sometimes at Harris's.' Harris's is the corner store. In the days before supermarkets, the corner store was where you got your groceries and your gossip. On Fridays you placed your weekly order with the store-owner, and his sidekick later delivered the groceries to your door in a wooden crate.

'I think she must be pretty smart', says my aunt, who will strike up a conversation with anyone. 'Name's Katya. Something like that. You should go and make friends. I know—kids your age don't like girls, do you? Well ... you'll learn', she says.

'Katya, huh?' I reply.

This plum that has fallen so fortuitously into my lap throws me into a dilemma. My first instinct is rush off and boast to Robbie. My more measured reaction is to keep the information to myself. The two impulses that rule my inner life—boasting and secrecy—are at war again. In the end, secrecy wins out. If he wants to, and if he's interested (something that I'm beginning to doubt), Robbie will have to seek her out himself.

One day, Robbie produces a ruler and suggests that we compare penises. 'I bet mine is longer than yours', he says.

That wouldn't be difficult, I think, but don't say anything.

'Look, look, it's at least half an inch longer', he announces triumphantly.

'You're stretching it.'

'If it was stiff, it'd be two inches longer. I bet you.'

———

I find myself riding my bike past her house several times a day and get to know its intricate external details, like the way the fly-wire screen enclosing the side verandah is lifting at the edge; the house bricks on the roof to stop loose sheets of iron from flapping in the wind; smoke curling from the kitchen chimney, even on the hottest day. The old man, presumably the grandfather, sitting in a sagging armchair on the front verandah for hours on end—white shirt, unbuttoned waistcoat, unlit pipe, gnarled stick between his knees.

To tell the truth, I feel slightly guilty; furtive even. These days I'd be called a stalker. Back then I was just a pervert. ('What are you perving at?' were fighting words at school and on the street.) Each day, I swear to myself that I'll go straight home after school, and each day my resolve crumbles as I pedal out of the school gate. I dawdle outside her house and then cross the street to knock on my aunt's door. My weekly visits to my aunt become daily ones, and she looks at me curiously as she hands me a cup of tea, but says nothing.

All houses in the town back on to a lane. The lanes are imaginatively named after the streets they follow. Beryl Lane follows Beryl Street. You will find Wills Lane wandering along behind Wills Street (one of the few streets in town named after an explorer rather than something you dig out of the ground). Each property comes to an end at the lane, with a corrugated iron fence, an outdoor toilet, and a gate. The night-soil cart, dunny cart, or shit cart— take your pick—trundles down the lane once a week to remove pans overflowing with putrid human waste and replace them with empty ones. I date my aversion to faecal matter in all its forms, from soiled nappies drying dog shit in the street, to the dunny man and his shoulder-hoisted, slopping pans.

One afternoon, my bike takes me down the lane behind her house. I stop and look over the corrugated iron fence that is coming adrift in parts. Someone has wired it up. I observe the neat rows of vegetables in the centre of the yard and the citrus trees along the side fence. There is nothing frivolous about this backyard. No flowerbeds. Not even a patch of lawn. Just the red dirt paths and the richly fertilised rows of vegetables.

Her face suddenly appears above the fence. Her large grey eyes look right through me. Her knuckles are white where they grip the fence.

'What do you want?' she hisses. Her voice is low, her peachy face white with fury.

'I ... I ...' I jump on my bike, and, face burning, pedal away as fast as I can, the burr of her accent ringing in my ears.

'I think I know where she lives', Robbie suddenly announces a few days later. My heart goes into free-fall. Since my unfortunate back-fence encounter with Katya, I've kept my distance. It's entirely possible that Robbie has been lurking round the neighbourhood as well.

'Bet you don't', I reply. The fact that it shouldn't matter

whether or not he knows is left unsaid. We both know that this is war.

'Do', says Robbie.

'Don't.'

'Do', he says again, and then adds, 'Fuck face.' Uncle Henry calls people 'Fuck face' all the time. I think it's meant to be funny.

'Where then?'

'Out the South.'

'Oh, yeah?'

'Yeah. She lives near my Aunt Sarge. I was down there the other day. I saw her.'

'Doesn't mean she lives there.'

'Does.'

While I'm happy that Robbie is off the scent, I feel the need to wrest back the initiative.

'Well, I know her name.'

'Don't', he says, scornfully this time, but leaves off the 'Fuck face.'

'Do.' Our testicles may have descended, and Robbie's voice at least had broken, but we were still capable of acting like five-year olds.

'So what is it?'

'Katya.'

'Katya?' He brushes a lock of dark hair out of his eyes. 'What kind of name is that?'

'Just a name.'

'So how do you know?'

'I just know.' Savouring my small victory, I jump onto my bike and ride away.

———

The next time I visit my aunt, I notice two rings hanging on lengths of ropes suspended from a branch of the large eucalyptus tree in front of the Khitrovo house. A young man wearing a white singlet and pair of grey pants comes out of the house and walks across to the tree. He stands motionless, contemplating the rings for a minute or two, then suddenly leaps into the air, grabs the rings, and swings himself into a perfect handstand. He stays there, motionless, for two or three minutes. The muscles in his arms and shoulders bulge, and the veins in his forearms and neck stand out like thick cords. Then he gracefully lowers himself and drops to the ground, brushes his hands on his pants and disappears through the fly screen door at the side of the house.

The following Saturday afternoon, I'm hanging out at the Police Boys' Club. The club has been established to keep us neighbourhood delinquents off the street and instil in us moral character by teaching gymnastics and getting us into the boxing ring where we can punch each other's lights out under the supervision of the local cop. I've arranged to play basketball with some of my friends, but it's fiercely hot, so we lurk indoors messing about on the trampoline. I've just mastered the back flip and am keen to show it off. You had to be careful to stay centred on the trampoline. Get to close to the edge, and you risked ending up like one of the Miller kids with a broken collarbone or worse.

I've just finished showing off to no-one in particular when Bernie, who lives next door to the club, says, 'Shit, look at that, would ya?' I flop onto the mat and look. On the far side of the gymnasium, Katya's brother is on the parallel bars. He has swung himself into a perfect handstand, legs together, toes pointing to the ceiling. That's no big deal (not that I could do it). Some of the older members of the club were pretty handy on the bars. But then the White Russian did something we had never seen before: He tilted his torso and legs to the left, changing his centre of gravity, and then lifted his right arm off the bar. He was standing *on one hand*. He stood there motionless for a minute or two and then lowered himself to the ground.

Emboldened, I go over to him and say, 'That was pretty good, mate.'

He gives me a gentle smile.

'Can you teach me how to do that?' He smiles again. I wonder if he understands a word I say. He stands there looking like movie star. The muscles of his upper body bulge. His frame tapers from the shoulders down to a slim waist and legs. The triangular shape of an elite athlete. His hair is darker that Katya's, but is still blond. Apart from a cow-lick on his forehead, his hair stays perfectly in place.

'What's your name?'

'Dmitri.'

'I know you. You live near my aunt.'

He just smiles again. I'm sure that he has no idea what I'm talking about. I turn to go back to Bernie when Dmitri speaks.

'Tomorrow, you come', he says.

I turn back. 'What? Here?' Then I remember. Tomorrow is Sunday and the club is shut. In those days, everything shut on Sunday—everything bar the pubs. When I impart this information, he simply says, 'My place.'

'So what did he say?' asks Bernie.

'His name's Dmitri.'

'Dmitri?'

'Yep. He's a White Russian.'

'A what?'

'A White Russian.'

'What's that when it's at home?'

'It's a Russian with white hair. Jeez, Bernie, don't you know anything?'

Later on Sunday morning, after Mass, I ride my bike down towards my aunt's house. But this time I ride on the other side of the road. From the Khitrovo household there is no sign of life. I loiter on the footpath, one leg hitched over the dinky bar of my bike. At least, for the first time, I have a legitimate reason for being here.

The screen door slams. Dmitri steps lithely off the verandah and comes towards me. He grins broadly and offers his hand, which surprises me. In our culture, only men shake hands, and I have yet to get used to the idea that I might be about to become one. I prop my bike in the gutter, and watch Dmitri as he jumps up, grabs the rings, and inverts himself with all the effort that it takes most people to climb into bed. He holds his pose for a minute before beckoning me.

'Now you!'

He puts his hands on my waist and hoists me upward. I grasp the rings and hang there. Dmitri demonstrates how to swing myself into an inverted position. I had always fancied myself as a gymnast and had reasonably well-developed arms and shoulders, but it takes all of my strength to invert myself, even with Dmitri's assistance.

I hold the inverted position for about twenty seconds, the muscles of my arms and torso shrieking. I hear the screen door bang. I maintain my pose for another ten seconds before dropping to the ground. Dmitri applauds and then claps me on the shoulder. I look towards the house. Katya is standing on the verandah, silently watching me. Dmitri, his hand still on my shoulder, leads me toward the verandah.

'My sister', he says.

'I know', I reply. I look her in the face, wondering whether she will slap mine or smile. From the way she looks at me, it could go either way.

'Hello', I venture.

'Hello', she replies, and then turns and disappears into the house. Dmitri follows her and returns with a jug of iced water and a couple of plastic mugs. We sit on the verandah sipping water, and then return to the rings. Dmitri gives me some tips on maintaining my balance while inverted, doing so through demonstration rather than explanation. It's all a matter controlling overbalance through pressure on the wrists and underbalance by bending the elbows slightly. The degree of over- and underbalance is microscopic. To the observer, the gymnast appears to be motionless, but in reality, he's working like hell. Occasionally, after many hours of practice, I achieve a state of perfect balance, and don't have to work my wrists and elbows. On the rare occasions that this happens, I feel weightless—in a state of perfect bliss. Years later I practice transcendental meditation in an attempt to achieve the state of mindlessness described by those who had been there, but the nearest I ever got to nirvana was the occasional perfect handstand.

At my second attempt, on this Sunday morning, I do better. I wonder whether Katya is watching through the lace curtains at the front of the house.

———

At that time, I had no idea what was happening to my body, in particular to my head and heart. One minute, for no apparent reason, my head would race and my heart would soar. I'd tear along on my bike singing wildly out of tune. Next thing I knew, again for no apparent reason, I would find myself face down on my bed, lost, bewildered, and depressed. It was at these low points that the priests made sense. They had an answer. This useless, futile life was a test bed for the next.

Particularly troubling were 'sex' and 'love'. In our house, both were four letter words, never to be mentioned. Once, to my extreme embarrassment and shame, my father came into the bathroom unexpectedly. I had just stepped out of the shower and was reaching for a towel. I don't know who was more embarrassed as he confronted the erection that was pointing in the approximate direction of his left shoulder. The erection and my dad stared each other down for a long minute before he threw me a towel and said severely, 'Cover up!' Then, almost kindly: 'Treat it with a cold spoon. And don't let your sister see it.' This was the beginning and end of my sex education.

I'm not sure whether the cold spoon cure was an effective treatment for rampant erections. I never took my dad's advice, preferring to deal with the problem not with a cold spoon, but a warm hand. In any case, the advice was hardly practical. Was I supposed to keep a spoon in the freezer for emergencies? How was I supposed to get from the scene of the crime to the kitchen to a private place where I could put my penis out its misery without drawing the attention of the rest of the family? What if, after repeated applications, my penis simply gave up, never to rise again? I could smuggle the spoon from the freezer to the bathroom before my shower, but how was I supposed to keep it cold? How cold did it have to be in order to be effective? And what about those other times during the day when, without provocation, my penis would spring into life? There were just too many uncertainties and imponderables to make the cold spoon a practical option. As a covert operation, it made kidnapping and espionage look like child's play.

One afternoon at school, we were handed envelopes to be taken home to our father, if we had one, and a responsible older male family member if we didn't. It was an invitation to a 'Father's and Son's Evening' at the local football club. That evening, I dutifully delivered the envelope to my father and watched as he tore it open and read the contents. Then he tore it in half and consigned it to the bin. That was the last of the 'Father's and Son's Evening' as far as he (and I) was concerned. I later learned that this event was a sex education 'seminar', although I never learned anything of the content. My classmates, notorious gossips and benders of the truth, never breathed a word of the event. How many of them (if any) went, I never found out.

And so members of the opposite sex entered my universe, most particularly the girl with the golden plait. Overnight, these loathsome creatures who just a year before were to be avoided at all costs became objects of desire. After school we would hang out on the corner up the street from the Convent, legs slung over the dinky bar of our bikes, pretending not to watch, but secretly evaluating and lusting over the girls as they rode home steadfastly ignoring us. We had our favourites. Ronnie was the universal object of desire. Tall and slim, she had fine white hair that was pulled back into a tight pony tail. She would sit demurely upright on her bike as she rode by, as cool as you like, even on the hottest day. She was the ultimate Ice Queen of our generation. As unapproachable and untouchable as royalty. It came as a considerable shock to us to learn one day that she had been sent away for an abortion.

I would have wildly uncontrollable dreams of extreme eroticism. Sometimes these involved Ronnie and some of the other Convent girls, but mostly they involved the girl with the golden plait. I would wake from a delicious dream to the cold disappointment of my bedroom and try to remove sticky evidence of shameful fantasies without waking my little brother who slept in innocent, pre-pubescent bliss on the other side of the room.

'Wet dreams?' said Robert, my knowledgeable older cousin. 'No big deal.'

Was it necessary to reveal them to the priest at Saturday confession?

'No need', he said.

Because they happened under cover of sleep, they were exempt from the status of mortal sin. Even priests had them. Even the Pope!

'No!' For some reason, I found this intelligence shocking.

Anyway, my cousin informed me, they were covered by the blanket formula we all used: 'Father forgive me for I have sinned. I had impure thoughts and deeds.' This covered everything from masturbation to lusting after Trudy Campbell's tits.

Most weekends, I would end up at Robbie's place. Being an only child, and motherless now to boot, he had a great deal of freedom. During the week, Uncle Henry spent his time at his car yard. On the weekends he spent his time with his mates in the pubs and clubs around the town.

Although Robbie had the run of the house and two rooms that were his exclusive preserve—his bedroom and his 'toy' room—he preferred to spend his time in his 'retreat' at the back of the yard. The retreat was a disused chicken coop. It was constructed of corrugated iron on three sides with chicken wire on the front. Robbie had put linoleum over the floor, which consisted of compacted earth and fossilised chicken shit. It was furnished with an old sofa and a folding card table. Pride of place on the table was a portable wind-up gramophone player. We would spend hours on a Saturday afternoon playing cards in the suffocating heat and listening to Johnny O'Keeffe, Col Joy and the Joyboys, and Little Patti, with the occasional Elvis platter thrown in for a bit of variety. I liked Elvis. Robbie preferred the Australian bands. He'd seen most of them live at Thebarton Town Hall when he visited his grandparents in Adelaide.

Just before Easter, his grandmother and grandfather, Gramp or Grampy (also known as 'Grumpy') came to visit. They brought the new skateboard with them. I was invited to Sunday lunch to admire this addition to Robbie's collection of toys, gadgets, games, and sporting gear. Gran bustled about the kitchen preparing the Sunday roast—a lump of mutton, peas, and roasted vegetables—potatoes, pumpkin, and parsnip. Uncle Henry and Grumpy sat at the kitchen table drinking bottles of West End beer. Robbie and I retreated to the chicken coop to listen to the new Elvis LP that had come with the skateboard.

When Gran called us from the back door to come to lunch, I excused myself and went to the spare toilet that adjoined the laundry at the back of the house. I had a need that had grown steadily in urgency and could be dealt with in only one way. It only took me a minute to attend to. I washed my hands in the laundry tub and entered the kitchen all ready for lunch.

'How was that?' asked Uncle Henry, and burst out laughing. It was clear that he'd had few.

'What?' I replied, mystified.

Robbie started laughing too. Even Grumpy gave a toothless smile.

'I told them you were out the back flogging yourself', said Robbie.

'Was... was not', I stammered, but my beet-red face gave me away. At that point even Gran laughed. Humiliated and shamed beyond belief, I forsook the roast mutton and fled the house vowing never to return. And I kept my promise all the way to Wednesday.

————

Dmitri continued to be my gymnastic mentor, giving me lessons two or three times a week. By now I was pretty accomplished on the roman rings. I could hold myself upright in a near perfect position; not as still as Dmitri, but getting there. My shoulders and biceps were beginning to develop, and I had much more strength in my upper body. Unfortunately, because of the short, stocky bicyclists legs I'd inherited from my grandfather, I would never have the classic gymnast's build.

Once Dmitri decided that I was ready to graduate from the roman rings, he produced a handstand set that he'd constructed himself. It consisted of a wooden base and two short pieces of waterpipe set into the base, which were topped by a pair of handpieces that Dmitri had carved from blocks of hardwood. He placed the handstand set on the footpath, grasped the handpieces, centred his weight over the set, and inverted himself slowly and seemingly effortlessly into a perfect handstand. Then he swayed his legs and hips leftward and raised his right arm until it was parallel to the ground. All of the movements were performed with the grace and ease of a professional athlete.

Then it was my turn. I grasped the handpieces, jerked myself upright, overbalanced, and ended up flat on my back on the footpath, the wind well and truly knocked out of my sails. When I'd recovered my breath, I tried again. This time Dmitri stood behind me and steadied my legs. He made me point my toes skyward, reminding me to find my centre of gravity with minute movements of wrists and elbows. Once I was balanced, he stepped away, leaving me balanced in a perfect handstand that I was able to hold for about a minute. In that minute, I came to see that gymnastics was as much about the mind as it was the body. You had to visualise perfection in order to achieve it. Building skills and bodily strength were means to an end that was something other than physical. The perfect handstand was a form of meditation.

Although I loved my sessions with Dmitri, I never lost sight of the fact that they were a means to quite another end. However, my pursuit of his younger sister made little progress. It was like stalking an elusive creature in the bush. Occasionally, as Dmitri and I went through our routines on the footpath in front of their house, she would appear on the verandah and watch us. However, as soon as my attention turned to her, she would fade away. She was a fantasy, playing at the edge of my vision and my mind.

———

One day, Grandpa Khitrovo crossed the road to my aunt's house and started restoring order to the shambling, overgrown mess that had once been a garden. My aunt tried to stop him.

'I can't afford to pay you', she said. He didn't speak a word of English. He gave her a toothless smile, ducked his head, and went on working. 'I hope he knows about the snakes', my aunt muttered darkly.

From then on, he crossed the road every day and worked on the garden. The only reward he sought was a mug of sweet, strong tea, which he drank standing up, tipping the tea into a saucer to cool before raising the saucer to his lips.

Grandpa always wore the same outfit: a pair of scuffed work boots, grey serge trousers held up with a piece of cord, a white shirt with sleeves rolled to the elbow, and a waistcoat. Even on the hottest day, he would toil under the relentless sun without removing his waistcoat. The only variation to his attire was a black beret, which he would wear on the hottest day and which was his only concession to the sun.

One afternoon, I noticed Dmitri and Grandpa sitting at the front of the house playing chess. I crossed the road and watched them. They played slowly and deliberately. The game was a mystery to me. At one point, Grandpa rubbed the side of his nose, made a rueful noise, stood up, and shuffled in to the house. It seemed that the game was over, although there were still chess pieces all over the board. The board itself was made from a solid piece of wood. The pieces appeared to have been carved from bone.

'You play', said Dmitri. I wasn't sure whether his state-ment was a question or a command. I took it as a question.

'Dunno how', I replied. Chinese checkers exhausted my board skills. To be honest, I found it difficult to sit still long enough to finish any kind of game. Sitting still was defi-nitely not one of my strengths. In class, I would sit squirming in my seat until the teacher glared at me and said something that he thought as suitably sarcastic such as, 'What's wrong with you? Got ants in your pants again?' For a while my nickname among my classmates was 'Ants'.

'I show you', said Dmitri.

Not wanting to offend him, I sat down in Grandpa's seat.

Dmitri set up the chess pieces and demonstrated the moves. Although his English was improving, it wasn't up to giving a verbal explanation of the intricacies of chess moves. And had he done so, I'm certain they would have defeated my powers of comprehension. Even after the demonstra-tion, I only had the foggiest idea of the moves. Also, I failed to see how a game could be won with opposition pieces still left standing.

Then we play a dummy game. Dmitri stays my hand as I'm about to make some monumental strategic blunder and places it on the piece I ought to move. As we play, Katya comes out of the house, perches on the edge of her broth-er's chair, and plays with his hair. Clearly, she adores him. I can feel the heat rising in my face and find it difficult to concentrate on the chessboard. Katya swings her leg to and fro. One of her sandals comes off and flies across the veran-dah. She giggles and runs to retrieve it. This lighter side of Katya is one I haven't seen before. Without the frown and slightly pouted lips, her face is transformed.

At the end of the game, which arrives quickly enough, I'm none the wiser about the whys and wherefores of the game.

Grandpa returns to the verandah and says something to Katya in what I take to be Russian. He hands her some money.

'I have to go up to the shops', she says to no one in particular, although the message could only have been directed to me.

'I'll come too.'

She shrugs and the frown returns to her face. 'If you want.'

Corner stores punctuate most of the neighbourhoods in the town. They are the lifeblood of the communities they serve. These days most have been driven to extinction by Big W, BiLo, and Coles, but back then they mattered. Most people made several trips a day to their local store: in the morning to buy bread and milk, in the afternoon for cigarettes, and in the evening for the daily newspaper and gossip. 'Did you hear about what happened to the Carters? Shocking about the Prescott girl, eh?' What the shopkeepers didn't know wasn't worth knowing. As kids, we were drawn like honeybees to the sweets counter, which was strategically placed at eye level, mesmerised by glass jars containing gobstoppers, mint leaves, liquorice straps, all-day suckers, and jelly babies. The candies gave the shop a sweet, musty smell.

We walk in silence. Katya is comfortable with the chirping crickets and the gum-nuts falling from the eucalypts. I'm in agony. I am desperate for words, but all I can think of is the inarticulate beating of my heart. This is the first time that I have walked shoulder-to-shoulder with the girl who has invaded my head. In fact, it's the first time I've walked shoulder-to-shoulder with any girl. There are alarming gaps in my knowledge. Where's the manual that tells you how this is supposed to work? Where's the script that tells you how it will play out?

As we trudge in silence, I steal an occasional sideways glance. Dust from the unpaved footpath has settled on the toes protruding from her open sandals. Her face, as ever, is impossible to read. There are no reciprocal sideways looks. She gives nothing away. Is she what Robert, my older cousin, calls an Ice Queen? I should ask for his advice. Girls are always hanging around him, so he must know something.

'For god's sake say something', I tell myself. It's like a mantra. But before I can dredge up a single inane thought we are at the corner store, and she is buying Grandpa his pipe tobacco. We return to her house cocooned in the same deafening silence that accompanied our walk to the store.

There is nothing more for me to do but take my leave.

'Guess I'll see you then', I say; my only words to her since inviting myself to accompany her to the shop. At that, she turns and looks me in the eye. It's an intense searching look, and, coward that I am, my impulse is to turn away. I hold her gaze for a minute, our faces inches apart, and notice for the first time that her grey eyes are faintly flecked with hazel. Then I swing my leg over the saddle of the bike and pedal slowly home.

I begin to despair of penetrating the protective wall that Katya has erected around herself. I still know next to nothing about her. Why was she, like her brother, not in school? What did she do in the great silence of that little house? What did she eat, what did she read, what did she think about? What colour were the walls of her room? Were they festooned with adolescent posters? Did she have little stuffed animals on her pillows like my female cousins? Did she have her period? What were her thoughts, dreams, and desires?

I knew more about her parents than I did about her: information gleaned through observation, deduction, and the occasional insight from Dmitri. Their mother left the house early each morning wearing the uniform of a hospital cleaner, walked two blocks to the bus stop, and caught the number 33 Hillside bus. She returned late in the afternoon on the same bus. Her father, who was an engineer by profession, worked as a labourer for the Water Board. The town was finally being sewered, and it was the immigrants who toiled in the heat digging trenches for the lines of concrete pipes that would carry our shit to god knows where, while their Australian bosses stood in the shade of the eucalypt trees drinking sweet black tea.

It was her grandfather who provided me with my best shot at advancing my cause, a cause I felt dying in my gut. Most afternoons he would appear at my aunt's place after lunch and work slowly and methodically at the vegetative mess that surrounded the house. Gradually, the tangle of creepers and encroaching saltbush were rolled back to reveal the archaeological remains of a once-substantial garden. Once the weeds, dead and dying shrubs, and other detritus had been removed, he took a pitchfork and began turning over the red earth, creating neat furrows that would receive seedlings in the coming planting season.

One day, while I was in the kitchen listening to *South Pacific* on my Aunt's little record player, the old man collapsed in the side garden. Although it was a school day, I had a heavy cold and had decided to give myself the day off. I'd said nothing to my mother and set off on my bike as usual as though I was going to school. However, at the corner I turned right and rode to my aunt's house. She was very relaxed about these things and was happy to have my company.

My aunt, sitting by the window with a cigarette hanging out of her mouth, saw the old man falter and fall. 'Quick!' she called. 'Go and see if anyone's at home across the road.' She rushed through the pantry and out the back door.

I ran in the other direction, panting heavily from my head cold. I bounded up the front steps of the Khitrovo house and banged furiously on the screen door.

The hallway inside the house is dark, silent, and deserted. I bang again and Katya appears, her golden hair slightly damp, floating across her shoulders. It's the first time I've seen her without her miraculous plait.

For the second time in our short acquaintance she says to me in her lilting, faintly lisping accent, 'What do you want?' This time, however, her tone is one of surprise, not scorn.

I'm about to speak, but am breathing so heavily from my heavy cold and recent exertions that the words won't come. I gasp for breath, and to my dying shame a gob of green snot shoots from my nose and hits the ground just inches from her unshod foot. We both stare down at the lump of mucus, she in surprise, me mortified beyond belief. Ignoring the lump of snot that lies dying between us, she asks again what I want.

Catching my breath, I say, 'It's Grandpa. He's ...'

Without waiting for me to finish, she slips into her sandals and rushes off across the verandah. She's wearing the little pair of red shorts she had on the very first time I saw her from the bottom of the drainage ditch. I dither. Should I remove the lump of snot or follow her? I leave the snot to shrivel in the sun and follow her down the steps. Guiltily, given the gravity of the situation, I notice the line of her briefs beneath her shorts.

We cross the street to my aunt's place. When we get there, Grandpa is sitting in the pantry happily slurping hot, sweet tea from a saucer. Katya falls on him and bursts into tears. He smiles faintly, pats her on the back, and looks contentedly into the middle distance.

———

Late one afternoon, Robbie drops by my house with big news. His Dad has bought one of the first television sets in town. The town itself did not yet have television, but the wealthier inhabitants were buying sets in preparation for its much anticipated arrival. This was due to happen later in the month via a set of repeater stations from Adelaide, thirty years after it had become part of the fabric of everyday life in the rest of the civilised world.

That evening, after I have finished my homework, I go over to Robbie's place to admire this latest acquisition. Some of the neighbours stand idly by watching Robbie's dad and uncle scrambling around on the corrugated iron roof as they attempted to attach a space-age antenna to the chimney. Inside, Robbie leads me proudly into the lounge room, where the television occupies pride of place, a blank green face enclosed in a mahogany box.

'Test pattern comes on at seven', he says.

For weeks before the service went live, those who had

purchased sets would switch them on at seven o'clock and watch the test pattern. Some even had test pattern parties. They would invite the neighbours around to drink beer and stare at the grainy grey-and-white pattern on the screen.

At 6.45 Robbie turns on the television. It takes several minutes for the set to warm up. The valves hum and emit a soft glow. Then the screen flickers into life, the screen transformed from inert green to pulsating grey-and-white flecks. The set emits a faintly hostile hiss. At 7.00 on the dot, the hiss fades and the flickering visual static is replaced by a test pattern that looks like a futuristic piece of art. We sit and stare at it in awe.

Robbie turns on the radio (or 'wireless' as it was known in those days) and tunes it to the local station so we have noise to accompany the electronic wallpaper we are staring at. The radio is a Bakelite affair that takes even longer to warm up than the television. Two radio stations are available to us. There's the regional ABC station that takes most of its programs as feeds from Sydney or Adelaide—compelling listening for teenagers such as *The Country Hour* and serials such as *Blue Hills* and *Dad and Dave*, programs so old that the characters get around in horse-drawn buggies and speak through their noses, a pre-war strategy adopted by country folks to avoid inhaling flies. The other station is 2BH, the local commercial station.

The radio is tuned to 2BH, which is owned and operated by an eccentric Englishman known as The Colonel. Broken Hill is populated by colourful characters—from Willie, the ex-Belgian mercenary to Harold, the one-armed handyman, to 'Pro' Hart, miner and primitive painter, to 'Uncle' Doc, master French polisher and terminal alcoholic who would restore furniture for a free Sunday roast. The list goes on. None was more eccentric than The Colonel, a large man with a handlebar moustache and an accent as rich as fruitcake.

Each evening at 7:00 p.m. The Colonel took over the microphone from Broken Hill's first and only DJ, the adenoidal Tony Tully. Tony had trained as a tea boy at a Melbourne radio station and thought of himself as cool. He was the first person in town to wear shoulder length hair, and he was trying to grow a goatee to hide his weak chin. The rest of the town thought him a fool. Whenever he showed up in one of the milk bars around town he was pilloried unmercifully. He referred to the audience, such as it was, as 'you cats out there in listening land' and used other expressions that even then were ten years out of date. However, he did manage to get his hands on music that even then was changing the rhythm of the world: The Beatles, Dylan, The Rolling Stones, The Moody Blues, and all the rest of them. My Dad, like most parents, loathed Tony, his music, and everything else he represented. 'Looks like a girl, with that hair', my father would mutter when he spotted Tony around town.

The Colonel had an easy listening program. Parents breathed a sigh of relief as the airwaves reverted to Frank Sinatra, Tony Bennett, and Rosemary Clooney, although the program was less about the music than about the Colonel. He would generously share with listeners stories of his day, read the occasional news item, and do all of the advertisements himself, reading the scripts in a dull monotone. Occasionally he would take callers. These were clearly stooges of his who would call up and ask leading questions, allowing The Colonel to drone on endlessly about himself.

Robbie does a great take off of the Colonel. He keeps

one eye on the test pattern in case suddenly, without warning, it might show signs of life, although there's actually more chance of life on Mars. Tonight is competition night on 2BH. The Colonel cons prizes out of his advertising sponsors and uses these to bribe his listeners. You never know what you might win. One night it might be a screwdriver set from Wood Sons The Hardware Specialists. Another night it might be a complimentary chicken chow mein from Lum Wah's Chinese Restaurant. Tonight the Hillside Theatre is offering two complimentary tickets to the opening night of their new movie. Well, it's new in Broken Hill; in the rest of the world it's been out for a couple of years. It is rather raunchily entitled *Lovers Must Learn*.

The Colonel explains how the competition works: He will pick a number at random from the telephone directory and dial it. To win the tickets, the person on the other end is supposed to pick up the receiver and say, 'Lovers must learn.' The Colonel must spend most of his spare time thinking up these nifty little competitions.

We listen to the rustle of the directory, the dialling of the phone, and the ring tone that goes on and on. Finally, the Colonel hangs up.

'Well', he says, his voice tinged with disappointment, 'must be out for the evening—unlucky folks.'

This procedure is repeated several times. Half the town is out on the town, or (unthinkable idea) have better things to do than tune in to *Easy Listening with the Colonel*. Finally, someone picks up and says, 'City Animal Refuge.'

'Sorry', says the Colonel, and cuts him off.

He sighs. The town has clearly disappointed him yet again. 'All right. Folks, this is your last chance.'

We half-listen to the Colonel dialling, and then suddenly the phone in the kitchen begins to peal.

'Shit!' says Robbie.

'Well, answer it.'

'You.'

'Me? It's your fucking phone. You answer it.'

'You. Go on. Quick. Before the Old Bastard hangs up.'

I go into the kitchen followed by Robbie. Heart thumping, I pick up the phone, and say, 'Lovers must learn.' I feel an utter fool. Thank God none of my classmates would ever tune in to the Colonel.

The Colonel is delighted. 'We have a lucky winner!' he says triumphantly. 'Well done, sir! And your name, if you don't mind?'

I mumble my name, which he makes me repeat and then spell out.

'Well, David, you can pick up your two complimentary tickets from our front office—any time during the next week. Enjoy the show. And remember folks, "Lovers must learn".'

I replace the receiver and a ferocious argument ensures. Robbie believes the tickets are his. 'It was *my* number the Old Bastard dialled', he says, 'not yours.'

I stand my ground. 'I did the dirty work. You didn't have the guts.' I settle the argument by saying, 'Well, I'm the only one who can pick up the tickets—they have my name.' Robbie concedes at that point. The fact that no one at the radio station knows me from a bar of soap doesn't appear to have occurred to him.

The following day at school is hell. All through the breaks, boys sidle up to me and whisper in my ear. 'Hey, Lover, what did you learn today?'

'Psst, Lover, what's one plus two?'

Even brats from the junior forms, who would never normally dare come near an older boy, were emboldened to pillory me. Only Bernie, who sat next to me in class, was sympathetic.

'What are you going to do with the tickets?' he asks.

'I'll think of something.'

Robbie thought that he had a moral right to at least one of the tickets. I had other ideas. That afternoon after school I scurried into town and picked up the tickets, figuring that I had certainly earned them.

My immediate challenge is how to approach Katya. I consult Bernie, the only one in the class who has a girl-friend. He comes in for constant ribbing, which he takes in his stride. He knows how envious we are—not that Sal, his girlfriend, is any oil painting. She's just a good-natured neighbourhood girl. Some Friday evenings, when his parents are at the pub for the night, Bernie asks us over to drink his dad's beer and play cards. 'So I don't do anything stupid', he says. Sal perches on the arm of his chair, watching the game with feigned interest and hoping like hell that we'll all go home so that she and Bernie can do something stupid.

After Bernie recovers from the surprise news that I'm actually interested in a girl, he says, 'You just have to ask her, mate. Make it sound like it's no big deal. Tell you what, if you go to the Saturday arvo show, Sal and me—we'll come too. You can tell your Sheila that a mob of us are going.'

I'm deeply suspicious of Bernie's strategy. However, no other option presents itself, and so the following afternoon when I know that Dmitri will be at the Police Boys' Club, I climb on my bike and pedal across to the Khitrovo House. My heart thumps. Feeling as though I'm about to undergo major surgery, and hoping like hell that neither of her parents is at home, I knock timidly on the side door. Katya eventually appears. She pushes the screen door open but doesn't step onto the verandah.

I plead my case as casually as Bernie had directed. Given the stakes, I feel anything but casual. She looks at me suspiciously for a moment, her grey eyes flicker, and then she gives the faintest of nods. I ride off, churning with conflicting emotions: euphoria fights fear, anticipation struggles with dread.

Bernie coaches me. He shows me how to feign a stretch, and then casually drop my arm across the adjacent seat. The hand then creeps forward until the outside of the thumb brushes her upper arm. The best time to make the move is during a dramatic moment in the film when she's likely to be distracted. It all sounds very clinical, but Bernie is the expert, and he has proof in the shape of Sal. The very thought of touching Katya's bare flesh brings a lump to my throat.

I offer to pick her up, but she says she'll meet me at the Hillside Theatre, which is opposite the Boys' Club, just a short walk from her home. The show starts at three o'clock. I meet Bernie and Sal at the milk bar next to the theatre. We drink lime spiders and play the pinball machine. Bernie is a pinball wizard. I suck. At 2.45, I buy a Cadbury's chocolate bar and stand on the pavement to wait for her. She turns up with her brother Dmitri and my heart sinks. Is he a chaperone? Apparently not. He gives me a wave and crosses the road to the Boys' Club.

She is a vision in white: white sleeveless top, white miniskirt, white sandals, and a little white handbag. Her hair is pulled back into a ponytail, which accentuates her

THE GIRL WITH THE GOLDEN PLAIT • 195

cheekbones and the line of her jaw and makes her look older. I offer her the chocolate bar, anxious to get rid of it before it melts. She drops it into her bag.

What do I do now? Take her hand? Better not. It isn't part of Bernie's script. Rescue arrives in the shape of Bernie and Sal, and I introduce them. I can tell that Bernie is impressed. He looks her up and down, touches her on the arm, which is more than I've ever done, and suggests that we go into the theatre.

The Hillside Theatre is old and ramshackle. Most of the horsehair seats are busted in one way or another, and many of the floorboards are loose. It burns to the ground several weeks later in a spectacular blaze that strongly suggests arson, a suggestion that the proprietor strenuously denies.

We find seats in an empty row towards the back of the theatre. Bernie and Sal occupy the seats next to the wall. Katya takes the aisle seat. I brush past her and take up the seat next to her. The back of the theatre is dotted with young couples, some of whom are already seriously at it. The younger kids sit at the front of the theatre. Once the lights dim, they throw Jaffas—hard, candy-covered choco-late balls—up the aisle, and laugh as the candies *kerplink-kerplunk* back down the steps to the front.

The main feature is preceded by Movietone News, a cartoon, and a Tarzan serial. Beside me, Katya is impassive. She neither laughs at the cartoons nor gasps at Tarzan's antics. Despite her brother's gymnastic prowess, swinging through the air with the greatest of ease is not something that rates with her. I can feel the heat from her arm. I can also feel the tension. Is she waiting for something to happen? Is she expecting it? Or dreading it? I steal a look at Bernie and Sal. He has one arm draped around her shoulder and one hand in her lap. Has Katya noticed? Does she get the idea?

After the serial, there is a short intermission. The younger members of the audience make a beeline for the exit. During the main feature, they'll steal cigarettes and run wild in the neighbourhood, returning to the cinema in time to be picked up by their parents.

Lovers Must Learn is a romantic comedy set in Rome. It stars a couple of clean-cut blond American actors called Troy Donahue and Angie Dickinson. I pay scant attention to the movie. I'm waiting for The Right Moment. Will I know when it arrives? One or two moments of what might be called dramatic tension come and go, but Katya doesn't seem to be particularly engaged by the film. Bernie turns his head in my direction. He has a get-on-with-it look in his eye. I feel just as I did when I tried out (unsuccessfully) for the school debating team. I raise my arm, feign a yawn, slump in my seat, and let my arm drop lightly on to the back of Katya's seat. She doesn't react, although the presence of my arm must surely not have gone unnoticed. Is this a good sign? Encouraged, I move my hand until my thumb brushes her upper arm. Then I curl my hand around her arm. *I have my arm around her.* She shrugs it off without taking her eyes off the movie. I retreat. Damn! What did I do wrong? Did I pick the wrong moment? If so, what constitutes a right moment? I have no idea. Did I move too fast? Maybe I should have let my arm rest on the seat until she'd got used to it.

At school, our English teacher would ask us what grade we expected before handing back our assignments. We would invariably should out 'A!' in unison. It had become a bit of a class joke. She would bat her eyelids, and intone

'Hope springs eternal in the human breast.' (A phrase I was later to learn she had stolen from Alexander Pope.) Our assignments, splattered in red ink, would come sailing through the air at us. The best any of us ever did was a B, although C was the default option.

It's less hope springing eternal than Bernie's eagle eye that impels me to try again. The casual flop strategy, which is meant to lead her to believe that the arm has landed on the back of her seat by a happy accident, clearly didn't work. This time it creeps around her like a furtive animal. I fully expect another shrug, or an angry 'What do you want?', but to my surprise she lets it remain. What now? I have finally executed Phase I, but Bernie never got around to coaching me on Phase II. Should I pursue the urge to stroke the fine down on her forearm? Almost certainly not.

Apart from allowing my hand to cup her upper arm, Katya gives no indication that anything has changed. She is as impassive as the Sphinx. I hardly expected a French kiss, but some kind of signal, the slightest movement of her shoulder in my direction, would have been reasonable compensation for a free movie ticket and a slightly limp bar of milk chocolate. But nothing. My arm might as well have belonged to someone else. Still, I have my arm around her. I'm touching her. Unfortunately, the moment doesn't last. My hand begins to sweat. Then it grows clammy, desecrating her warm, dry flesh. At that she shrinks away, imagining perhaps that my hand has morphed into a giant, slimy mollusc. I have no option but to beat a retreat.

Afterwards, she is kind enough to let me walk her home. As we leave the theatre, Bernie gives me a not-so-discreet thumbs up. At the entrance to the Khitrovo property, where the front gate would have been, if they'd had a front gate, she says goodbye and thanks me, making it clear that this is as far as I was going to get. As she reaches the verandah, she turns and give me the faintest of enigmatic smiles. I go home happy, carrying the smile like a kid with a Violet Crumble bar.

Most of us remember our first love, often dismissively referred to by others as a 'crush' or 'puppy love'. As I was about to be tipped over from my teen years to my twenties, I once unwisely confided to my father that I was 'in love'. Never one to leave you in any doubt as to his own opinion, he replied brusquely: 'You're only twenty. You wouldn't know what love is!' I never did figure out at what age one was licensed to love. For me, my first love, first crush, call it what you will, signalled the seismic shift from childhood to adolescence. This shift happened without any conscious effort on my part. And try as I might at times, there was no going back. Even though my voice had still not broken, I was on a one-way trip and had passed the point of no return.

Seeing members of the opposite sex as objects of desire rather than creatures to be exterminated is only one indication of the onset of adolescence. Another is that on rare family outings, I take to walking several steps behind my parents, pretending to be someone else's son. Also, despite having smoked since the age of nine, I actually begin to enjoy the taste of cigarettes.

While the metamorphosis from childhood to adolescence in inevitable, irreversible, and happens whether we like it on nor, the next stage—from adolescence to adulthood—involves a conscious decision and considerable effort over time. Many of us decide that the rewards are not worth the struggle and settle for a lifetime of adolescence: fine for us, but hell for those around us.

———

And so to the happy ending of this tale. Picture me sitting with Katya in the privacy of the Khitrovos' back porch. We're home alone, out heads bent over Dmitri's chess set. She moves her queen and I'm hopelessly in check. It's now-or-never time. I lean across the board and our lips touch. Lips locked, we stand and press our bodies together. My hand moves up her firm brown leg, comes to the hem of her cotton briefs, and continues up and over the mound of her buttock.

In your dreams, mate! And it's in my dreams that my first love begins and ends. I'm about to learn that this is not the way of the world. Well, maybe it is for the lucky few like Bernie.

My dream ends late one afternoon as summer begins to falter. Despite the growing warmth of our relationship; despite my promises to myself; despite faint feelings of guilt, I find myself riding slowly past her house, which appears to be deserted apart from a three-speed Skid Kid propped against the front fence.

With a sense of foreboding, I ride to the end of the street, turn left, and make my way up the lane toward the scene of my first close encounter and my shame. I glance over the fence and there she is, standing in the shade of the large lemon tree whose fruit is about to set. She is not alone. Robbie has her in his arms. Their lips lock. As his hand makes its way up her firm brown leg, I pedal slowly on.

I have no reason to return to that part of town. My aunt has moved to Adelaide for an extended stay to look after a second cousin who is recovering from cancer. And Dmitri? The gymnastic lessons? The interminable games of chess?

The last I hear of Dmitri is on the local radio. I'm sitting in the kitchen eating toast and marmalade. The Colonel is reading the morning news.

'One person is dead following an accident on the Menindee Road in the early hours of this morning. The deceased has been identified as Dmitri Khitrovo, 20, of Railwaytown Broken Hill. Two other passengers are in a critical condition in the Broken Hill and District Hospital. The driver of the vehicle, who has not been identified and who escaped serious injury, is helping police with their inquires.'

The accident occurred two miles from the Quandong Hotel, when the car left the road and rolled over.

I've made my peace with Robbie, although I see less and less of him as he cultivates other interests. He and Bernie, who had been rivals all through school, spend a lot of time together. I see them now and then down Argent Street, with Sal and Katya, drinking lime spiders in the Orange Spot café.

Robbie tells me about Dmitri. He suffered a broken neck and died instantly. When they lifted him out of the car, there was not a blemish on his perfect body, and his hair was still in place.

MARY'S BOY

The first words he ever said to me were 'You're Mary's Boy.' It was less a question than an assertion.

I was.

'Right', he said. 'I'm ready.'

He was smaller than I'd expected, although in relation to his frame he had a large head that was piled with thinning yellowish hair. It was midsummer and hot, but he wore a seersucker jacket, which he kept on all day, and a pair of grey flannel pants with a defective zipper that had positioned itself at half-mast.

The most striking aspects of his appearance were his eyes—pale, wet, and penetrating—and his voice, a conscious baritone that hardly fitted his body. He walked like a pouter pigeon, his chest pushed out and his chin held high, as though he had something to prove.

I'd been worried about what to talk about on the ninety-minute drive. I needn't have been. He kept up a rich, rolling monologue, ranging over an enormous number of subjects from Italian art to the scandal of pop music (I couldn't quite see the connection, but he attributed many current ailments in the art world to the latter) to the origins of the Australian accent. He also overestimated my state of knowledge, and the monologue came at me through bursts of intellectual static (What was a triphthong? Why was it obvious that Michelangelo's David was blatantly pederastic?) Following his mental grasshoppering as well as trying the keep the car on the road and heading in the right direction ('Go south', they said. 'You can't miss it.') placed a serious burden on my powers of concentration.

Mostly he talked about himself. 'They affect to despise me', he said. 'Call me the writer chappie with the Wog wife. But principally, they're afraid of me.' I had no idea who 'they' were, but had no intention of interrupting him. I later learned that he was the one who did the despising. He was a great hater, and professed a detestation of 'Englishness', if not of England itself. He was pilloried by the English press when he decided on self-exile in Malta.

'One hack called me a "rat leaving a sinking ship". Well, weren't rats wise to leave sinking ships?' He said the only guilt he felt at leaving England was the guilt of not missing it.

Tiring of his theme, or perhaps sensing my distraction, he turned his attention to Australia. Although he had only been in the place for five minutes, he had its measure. The problem with Australia was that it had inherited the worst that British colonialism had to offer—prudery, anti-intellectualism, a determination to pillage and rape. 'Look at this', he said, with an expansive sweep of his hand. We had passed beyond the city and the suburbs and were heading through rolling hills white with dusty summer wheat towards wine country. 'You live in this marvellous place, but you don't love it. Now, who said that?'

I had no idea, but didn't have to wait to be enlightened.

'Lawrence. David Herbert. His is still the only decent novel ever written about your country. And the only truly great novelist you've ever produced, Patrick White, is more English than the English. There's no *originality*.' The yellow stuff on his head trembled. No, the place was doomed from the moment it was colonised by the British.

A ruminative pause, then: 'Of course, I'm a composer really. Writing, well, it isn't a sideline of course, but it's my music that I'll be remembered for. I'm working on my third symphony right now.' There was another silence, this time for a minute or two, and then suddenly, unexpectedly, he broke into song. I had no idea what the song was, as it was in Italian, but his baritone voice sounded marvellous.

He seemed in good humour on the drive—nothing of the reputed surly misogynist about him. It may have been that the white light and the Mediterranean hills with their olive groves and arcs of vineyard reminded him of his adopted home. It may have been the prospect of a day of pleasure.

Finding the winery wasn't difficult. The town only had one main street, and Hardy's winery was the largest enterprise in town. On arrival, we were met by the other celebrated guests and numerous members of the Hardy family. These included Frank—later to become Sir Frank Hardy for his services to yachting. (What would Burgess have made of that?) Also in the party was an elderly member of the family whom everyone called 'Uncle Tom'. We were taken to a massive barn where hundreds of wine barrels were stacked from floor to ceiling. Inside the barn it was cool. A sweet, rotting smell seeped from the barrels. Through the dim light, I could see that trestle tables had been set with food and wine at the rear of the barn. 'This looks promising', said Burgess, rubbing his hands.

'Good', said Mary, resting a motherly hand on my shoulder. 'You got him here. Well done!' Burgess was immediately swept away and I was left, hero no longer, standing by the doorway.

———

As I grew through adolescence, the town seemed to shrink. Its parochialism depressed me. The umbilical cord holding me to the place got tighter and tighter until one day it snapped. I wasn't sure where I wanted to be. Anywhere but here.

Reading was a solace and a torment. Books offered a means of escape. They opened up alternative worlds of exotic possibility, but they also rubbed my nose in the dirty reality that, in a practical sense, there was really no escape. School was over, and all that lay before me was an interminable summer of suffocating heat, red sand, and flies. Although my parents had made it clear that they couldn't afford the fees and the upkeep, I had sent off applications to universities in Sydney and Adelaide. Something would turn up—a scholarship, a student loan. I would study part time and find work. First, however, a university had to accept me.

I belonged to the central municipal library as well as the library at my father's club, and spent several hours each day at one or the other. I also had an informal book exchange with Johnny, the only other boy I knew who saw reading as a serious pursuit. Johnny's parents had money. Well, his grandfather had money, which was drip-fed down to the rest of the family. He was able to buy any book he wanted, and one wall of his bedroom was covered in book-crammed shelves. Johnny was an only child, and a genius, apparently. His application to study arts/law had been dispatched and returned almost immediately with a provisional acceptance, pending the results of the Higher School Certificate. His future was assured. Each day, I rushed to the mailbox once the postman had been. Bills and Christmas cards were the extent of his largess. Nothing for me.

Occasionally, for variety, I visited suburban branches of the central library. However, I never went back to the one around the corner. Occasionally, I spotted the librarian in the street and avoided him. Seeing him brought back memories of that shameful afternoon several years before.

I was an omnivorous reader, although not a particularly discriminating one. I had graduated from Enid Blyton, of course, but continued to read Agatha Christie and Leslie Charteris. Ian Fleming had also entertained me for hours on end. I devoured each James Bond adventure as soon as I could get my hands on it and fantasised about Monte Carlo, martinis, fast cars, and scantily clad women. In my final year at school we had read *The Power and the Glory*, and I sought out other books by Graham Greene. Johnny, who had a slight trace of European blood somewhere in his genealogy, tried to turn me on to French and Russian literature. Proust I found impossible to read, but I loved Dostoyevsky's *The Idiot*. It was also Johnny who introduced me to contemporary novelists such as Anthony Burgess. 'I want *The Malaysian Trilogy* back, but you can keep this one', he said, tossing me *A Clockwork Orange*. 'It's ridiculous.'

I started writing as soon as I could hold a pencil. It was a struggle, but a pleasurable one. Over the years, the pile of notebooks and foolscap pads on the cheap veneer desk beside my bed grew ever higher. I entered competitions at school and elsewhere, and even won a few, which was a source of immense pride.

One year, I snatched victory from the female literary types at the convent school for an essay on the Blessed Virgin Mary. At a lunchtime ceremony, none other than the Bishop presented me with my prize, a large garish painting of the Lady herself, which my mother insisted on hanging over my bed.

First prize in a competition sponsored by the RSL (the Returned Servicemen's League) was a lurid and no doubt historically inaccurate account of a First World War battle. The essay gained me an entry in the state final that, to my disappointment, I failed to win. The piece was based on the exploits of the Light Horse Brigade—a pastiche of anecdotes by one of my great uncles who had served in the Great War. At the end of the war, Great Uncle Reg had been ordered by his British commander to hand over his horse to be shipped back to England, where it would be sent to the glue factory. Reg shot his beloved horse and was lucky to escape being court-martialled.

In early summer, Johnny passed me a cutting from a magazine to which he subscribed. It was a call for applications to a Young Writers' Forum to be held in conjunction with the Writers' Week Festival in Adelaide.

'Why don't you apply?' he asked me.

'Why don't you?'

Johnny sniffed. He had moved on from literature and notions of being an author. His sights were now set much higher: on a career in law or politics, or possibly both.

I sent off my application, along with extracts from an unpublished (and unpublishable) novel, and, apart from an acknowledgement, heard nothing. Assuming that I'd been unsuccessful, I put the forum out of my mind. Boys from Broken Hill didn't win these kinds of awards. They went to sophisticated, city types.

Then, one day, unexpectedly, a letter arrived:

Congratulations. You have been selected to present your work at the Young Writers' Forum at the upcoming Writers' Week Festival in Adelaide. While we are unable to underwrite your travel costs, we are pleased to provide you with accommodation in the halls of residence at the University of Adelaide.

The only two commitments that the 'young writers' had during Writers' Week were to give a public reading of our work and to accompany a 'real writer' on a series of school visits. The other 'young writers' turned out to be considerably older than me. Most were in their thirties, a good ten to fifteen years older than me. The major criterion for applying for the Young Writers' Fellowship was that one be unpublished but 'show promise' (a quality that remained undefined and largely invisible throughout the week). In later years, one or two of the awardees, me included, staggered into print, but most disappeared without trace.

The invitation came quite late. In fact, Writers' Week was due to begin in a little over a week. In retrospect I realised that I must have been a late acceptance, that I had benefited from a drug overdose or the death of someone's aunt. At school, I was the perennial first reserve on the football team. Now it seemed I was destined for a similar role on the literary scene. I didn't care. I was in.

Hot on the heels of the award came a provisional offer of a place at university in Sydney. It was provisional because I had not quite accrued the requisite number of points for a place and had to take a supplementary exam. If I was interested in the offer, I was to complete and return a form that was included along with the offer letter, and present myself at the university at the end of the month.

These two offers represented my ticket out of the pokey, provincial hole that Broken Hill had become to me. The only problem was that I was flat broke. I didn't even have the cash for a bus ticket to Adelaide. However, I was on a lucky streak. An uncle was on his way to Adelaide that very weekend, and was happy to give me a ride. From there, I'd be on my own. Although he made me a bit uncomfortable, this uncle, with his prolonged silences punctuated by penetrating and often confrontational questions, I didn't mind. I was going to perform at Writers' Week, I was going to rub shoulders with people who could walk into bookshops and libraries and see their names on the spines of books. It made me giddy. The fact that I was broke and that I knew no-one in Adelaide were of little moment. I wasn't even sure where my promised accommodation was to be found, but that didn't matter. I was on my way to Writers' Week.

I was up at dawn on Sunday morning. My mother made me eat breakfast. 'Who knows when you'll have a decent meal again?' was her motherly question when I sniffed at the bacon and eggs. Then, slinging over my shoulder a duffel bag stuffed with several t-shirts, pants, a spare pair of Levi's, and several of my precious notebooks, I made my

way through the side gate and sat in the gutter, my back
against the ghost gum on the corner, waiting for my uncle.

———

The person I was most anxious to see, if not to meet, was
Anthony Burgess. *A Clockwork Orange* still coursed through
my veins. More than any of the other recent stuff I'd read, it
had changed the way I looked at literature. To that point, I
had struggled with a disjunction between the 'high culture'
enshrined in the kinds of novels I had been reading and the
popular culture that suffused all other aspects of my daily
life—the music, the movies, and even the poetry. How was
it possible to weave Led Zeppelin, faded Levi's, and incense
into writing in a way that made sense? How could I create
convincing characters who would rather consume dope than
fine wine, whose dream was to sit cross-legged on a hilltop
in Nepal?

Looking back, I see I was naïve, and poorly read to
boot. I hadn't read *Last Exit to Brooklyn* (banned in Australia
at the time) and had only just embarked on the Beats. But
I'd read *A Clockwork Orange*, and it opened all sorts of doors.
For a neophyte writer, it made things possible in ways I had
never imagined. Its author was a cult figure to me and, as I
was to discover, to the few of my fellow literary aspirants
who had read it. And now I was on my way to see him. It
was only later I discovered that he despised pop culture in
all of its manifestations.

Physically, Adelaide was tidy, small, and smug. A university, art gallery, museum, and library sat cheek by jowl in the
centre of town. The student accommodation to which I was
allocated was in a Catholic college (was there no escape?) on

a hill in North Adelaide overlooking the Torrens River and the Adelaide Oval. The room was spartan, but contained everything I needed.

The public reading took place at the Adelaide Museum and Art Gallery in a small room (clever that!) with oak panels. There were eight of us, and about thirty people in the audience. The program had me listed as sixth. The other literary hopefuls were novelists and poets, with one children's author thrown in for good measure. One was an overweight individual in his early thirties who had long hair and a beard and who concealed his bulk beneath a caftan. The others were women. We were introduced to each other by the organiser, and made polite noises to each other until the event began. One of the poets announced that she had just had a poem accepted for publication by her local newspaper in its Saturday Arts page. She was publicly congratulated and secretly envied.

I had memorised a page or two from my dreadfully overwritten, adolescent novel and delivered it nervously to a politely attentive audience. Afterwards, over coffee and biscuits, a smartly dressed middle-aged women approached me and made some nice noises about my piece. I don't recall exactly what she said, although the faintly damning 'promising' was mentioned more than once.

'I'm Mary', she said. 'Some of us are meeting for drinks at six o'clock. The balcony bar at the Hotel Richmond. Why don't you join us? I think you'll find it amusing.'

She turned out to be Mary Durak, one of the keynote speakers for the week. She had produced a defining work of her generation—a memoir of her landowning family called *Kings in Grass Castles*. I had studied it in school. It was one of the few set texts that I had actually enjoyed.

I earned the soubriquet 'Mary's Boy' from Hal Porter. Like Burgess, Porter had thinning, yellowish hair. Unlike Burgess, he had an aquiline face that was permanently flushed and a long thin frame. Although he had made his career as a playwright, he was at the height of his fame with a memoir called *The Watcher on the Cast Iron Balcony*—a wonderful title. Unfortunately, the title was the best part of the work. Porter disappeared from the scene for many years, and then one day I came across a brief paragraph in a national newspaper reporting that 'celebrated author Hal Porter' had been fatally struck down by a car as he was crossing the street in a small Victorian town.

Mary's invitation was kind, but I had no intention of taking her up on it. She and her colleagues were celebrities; they were the centrepiece of the Writers' Week festival. I was a nobody, a watcher from my own cast iron balcony. However, at six o'clock, I decided to walk by—mainly to see if I could spot Burgess. The Balcony bar was on the first floor of the Richmond Hotel. It looked down onto Rundle Street, the main shopping street, which would one day be turned into a mall, when such things became mandatory in cities and towns across Australia.

Mary was sitting with a several middle-aged people. She saw me, as I'd half-hoped she would, and called me over. The people she introduced me to included Hal Porter, the Irish novelist Edna O'Brien, and the Chief Justice of the state, John Bray, who was also a gifted poet.

These were the days when South Australia, effectively a city-state consisting of Adelaide and little else except thousands of square miles of empty semi-desert, was flourishing as a centre of the arts and liberal thought. Led by the charismatic politician Donald Dunstan, it had the most liberal laws in Australia on things such a marijuana use and homosexuality. Equal opportunity and labour laws were more advanced here than elsewhere. The Adelaide Festival of Arts was a glittering cultural event in a physical desert. South Australia was home to a wine industry that was about to be discovered by the rest of the world. And, although Dunstan is long gone, the restaurant scene that flourished under him (Dunstan himself had a restaurant) remains and rivals that of much less provincial cities internationally.

Not everybody had a charitable view of Adelaide. A friend once said, 'You'll only fit in there if you wear a pink shirt and call yourself "Jeremy".' Years later, Salman Rushdie, centrepiece of a later Writers' Week, called it truly the most evil place he'd ever been in. I wonder whether subsequent events in his life ever prompted him to revise his opinion.

Mary asked me what I wanted to drink. 'Beer, please', I said. The others were drinking white wine. Mary went to find a waiter. While she was gone, a small man wearing a suit, in spite of the heat, and carrying a cane with an ornate silver knob came and sat at the table. After he had greeted the others, he turned to me. 'And who are you?' he asked.

I hesitated just long enough for Hal Porter to say, 'This is Mary's Boy.' There was a rumble of laughter around the table.

This character was Max Harris, a bookshop owner, author, and the convener of Writers' Week. I had never heard of him, and only subsequently discovered what a significant figure he was—that although he never established a name for himself as a creative writer, he had been a pivotal character on the arts scene for many years. In the 1940s he published a magazine called *The Angry Penguins* and then established a movement of the same name whose members included the artists Arthur Boyd, Albert Tucker, and Sidney Nolan.

Harris and the Angry Penguins were responsible for the greatest literary hoax in Australian letters. They claimed to have discovered a 'primitive' poet, Ern Malley, whose sister had sent Harris a manuscript she discovered after her brother, a mechanic, died from a rare disease. Two volumes of poems were published, each with introductions by Harris, and they were hailed as works of genius. The literary establishment lauded the discovery and heaped praise on the poems. It also caused a huge literary stink when it was discovered that the poet and his work had been created by Harris and friends.

Had the group emerged in the 1970s, they would have been given the label 'alternative'. Their function was to 'stick one up' the conservative literary and academic establishment—which they successfully managed to do with their Ern Malley hoax. By choosing Angry Penguins, an incongruous, even contradictory adjective / noun combination, for their name, they presaged a style to be adopted by rock groups from the psychedelic seventies to the present day—from Iron Butterfly to Savage Garden.

Harris asked Edna O'Brien if she were ready for her evening performance. Each of the invited writers had to do one major public presentation, and it was her turn tonight. 'I hope so', she said. She had high cheekbones and piercing eyes and spoke in a rich Irish brogue. Her hair was kept in place by a colourful bandana. I thought that she was very exotic, and wondered what her writing was like.

Mary Durak came back with a waiter who carried a tray with another bottle of wine and a glass of beer. The group traded anecdotes and gossip. I had no idea who they were talking about, but was thrilled to be part of this sophisticated group. After a while, Max Harris took Edna O'Brien away so that she could prepare for her evening performance. A lesbian couple took their place. Everyone seemed to know everyone else.

Much of the buzz was about Burgess. He was considered 'risky', prone to arrogance and temper tantrums. 'Still, if we ruled out everyone with egos and tempers, we wouldn't have a Festival.' Much laughter again.

Burgess was a cult figure to me and those of my generation who still bothered to read. While it was his earlier work, particularly the Malayan trilogy, that had made him famous among the older generation, it was *A Clockwork Orange* that resonated with us. Not long after the Writers' Week Festival, the film of the same name was released amidst huge controversy and critical acclaim, and Burgess became something of a literary superstar. At the time of the festival, however, he was still relatively unknown to the general public.

At this point, I still hadn't laid eyes on Burgess. I asked Mary where he might be, but she was vague. 'Oh, you can never be sure. He's very hard to pin down.' Later she told me that she expected him to be at the opening of an art exhibition in a private gallery on North Terrace, not far from Elder Hall, where most of the Writers' Week events were being held. There was to be a cocktail party prior to Edna O'Brien's speech, and she expected that everyone would be there. 'You'll need this', she said, handing me an invitation. 'And it wouldn't hurt if you smartened yourself up a little.'

I 'smartened myself up' by exchanging my t-shirt and

jeans for a crumpled shirt and pair of pants. Then I went to the cocktail party. No one asked me for the invitation, but I had to put my name on a list. As a result, I received invitations to all sorts of receptions, and for the rest of the week, I thrived on sparkling wine, cheese, and biscuits. If this was bohemia, I was all for it.

After I had signed in to the reception, I clung to the wall, glass in hand. No one bothered me. No one paid me any attention. I piled a plate with food. I helped myself to a handful of cigarettes (the exhibition and reception were sponsored by a tobacco manufacturer). Burgess was nowhere to be seen.

After a time, Hal Porter appeared. He was wearing a white linen suit and seemed a little unsteady on his feet.

'Getting everything you need? Everything you want?'

'Have you seen Burgess?' I asked.

'Ah, Burgess!' He sniffed and disappeared into the milling crowd in the centre of the room.

At eight o'clock, the food disappeared and the drinking stopped. It was time to go and listen to Edna O'Brien. Elder Hall, on the grounds of Adelaide University, was packed. Max Harris presided over the event. He cut a curious figure on the stage. Seated at the table, all that was visible to most of the audience was his head and the knob of his walking cane. Edna O'Brien still had the bandana on her head. She also wore a caftan, which made her look even more exotic. After Harris had introduced her, she spoke on 'Women in Irish literature'. The audience loved it. It was my first direct brush with feminism.

Later, in the crush of the foyer, as I struggled to get a drink, Mary Durak pulled me aside. She asked me if I had a driver's licence. I did. She had a favour to ask. Next day there was to be a lunch to honour the main Writers' Week speakers. It would be held at a winery in McLaren Vale, a wine-growing district south of the city. The speakers were being bussed down, but Burgess had to do an interview in the morning. Could I possibly drive him down after the interview? I could. Good. I was to pick up Mary's car from her hotel and then pick up Burgess from his hotel at twelve o'clock.

'How will I know him?' At that time, I didn't even know what he looked like.

'Oh, you'll know him.'

———

Like many wine-growing families in South Australia, the Hardys were from German stock. At the time of the literary festival, two elderly aunts, who spoke no English, were visiting from Germany. They sat quietly in a corner of the room clutching glasses of wine. At one point Burgess went over and spoke to them in German. They seemed delighted. Burgess himself seemed relaxed and happy. I watched him as he worked his way around the room. At one point a tiny dark-haired woman with massive breasts became attached to him. When his progress around the room brought him close to me, he introduced her to me as Liana, his wife.

The food was finished, but the wine corks continued to pop. Burgess banged on a table.

'Time to repay our hosts', he declared. The deal was that everyone had to perform. Not me, surely! I was just the driver.

Burgess adopted a Napoleonic pose, with his hand stuck

in his shirt front, and recited Andrew Marvell's great seduc-
tion piece *To His Coy Mistress*.

> *Had we but world enough, and time,*
> *This coyness, lady, were no crime.*
> *We would sit down, and think which way*
> *To walk, and pass our long love's day.*

And later in the poem, tellingly:

> *... worms shall try*
> *That long preserv'd virginity,*
> *And your quaint honour turn to dust,*
> *And into ashes all my lust.*
> *The grave's a fine and private place,*
> *But none I think do there embrace.*

Then the elderly aunts sang some German folk songs,
accompanying themselves on odd-looking stringed instru-
ments. The others sang or recited bits of poetry and prose,
and all in all it was a jolly afternoon. At the end of the
performances, Uncle Tom gave everyone a bottle of Hardy's
wine. I got one as well, even though I hadn't performed.

When it was time to leave, Mary ushered Burgess and
Liana towards the bus. Burgess was about to clamber on
board when he noticed me looking rather forlornly at the
departing group. 'I'll go back with Mary's Boy', he said.
'Can't have the chap driving back alone.'

On the drive back I asked him what he was working on.
'I'm having a difficult time with a chap called Kubrick', he
said. 'He doesn't like my script. He doesn't like anybody's
script. Problem is, I don't think he understands the book.'

'What book is that?' I asked.

'*A Clockwork Orange*. What other work of mine would Kubrick film? Thing is, he thinks it's about violence.'

'What is it about?' I asked, not letting on that I had read it. Like Kubrick, I was also under the impression that it was about violence.

'Well, it's about language as much as anything. But a film is made from images, not from words. I'm worried about this film. I don't think it's going to do me any good.' He looked at the late Sunday afternoon traffic and said, more to himself than to me, 'I can't understand why I wasn't asked to write the music score.'

Back at his hotel, Burgess asked me to wait. He disappeared inside and reappeared a few minutes later with a book which he inscribed to me. I was disappointed to discover it was not one of his own works, but a compilation of verse. Still, it was kind of him, as indeed, it had been kind of him to forsake Liana of the generous bosom to accompany me back to the city. My compensation, when I got to look through the book, was that it contained *To His Coy Mistress*, with margin notes by Burgess.

The day after the winery picnic was school visit day. Each of the Writers-in-Waiting was paired with one of The Greats, presumably to give the school kids a look at the promise as well as the reward. I was paired with a local Adelaide writer, Colin Thiele, who wrote books for adolescents as well as historical and autobiographical pieces. Several of these later made their way on to the screen, which made him something of a minor celebrity. He was quiet, polite, and looked like a barber. Someone else got Burgess, much to my disappointment.

We were driven to a suburban high school, and the

reading was held in the auditorium in front of the senior school. At that time, I had never heard the phrase 'working the audience'. I doubt that it had even been coined. But that's what Colin Thiele did, in his own quiet way. He gave a narrative of his life that was full of funny stories, interspersed with short readings from his works. The high school kids seemed to enjoy it. I did my set piece from the Writers' Week event, and there was polite applause. Then a teacher—it must have been the head of the English department—made a speech while I sat on the stage and looked at the pretty, upturned faces in the front row. Then we were asked to recite something else. Colin Thiele told a story about his boyhood. Riskily, I read *To His Coy Mistress*. As we were leaving the school, a bevy of girls asked Colin to sign copies of his new book. Then two of them shoved dog-eared exercise books at me and asked me for my autograph.

―――

In my short time with him, Burgess was unfailingly polite to me—a cross between a kindly, if somewhat testy, uncle and patronizing older brother. The only time he directed any real venom at me was when I admitted that I liked pop music. He railed at me for several minutes about gibbering illiterates with their unspeakable noise. I was surprised, naively thinking that the author of *A Clockwork Orange* must be sympathetic to the current generation of youth and its preoccupations. Of course I had completely missed the point. I had not yet read *Enderby Outside*, in which he created a savage parody of John Lennon and his pretensions as a poet. The assassination of the Lennon character at a pivotal point in the book turned out to be remarkably prescient when, a decade later, the real John Lennon met the same fate.

———

Not long ago, I read a new Burgess biography. The author portrays his subject as an egotistical, vitriolic egomaniac. There's no doubt that he thought extremely well of himself. However, to suggest, as this book does, that Burgess had no redeeming features as a writer and few as a human being is wrong. As I closed the book, I wondered why someone would spend years researching and writing about someone they loathed but whom they had never met.

A LONG WAY BACK

When I had finished these pieces, I had a powerful urge to return to Broken Hill. 'What was it like?' my daughter had wanted to know. As I neared the end of my writing journey, a similar question kept surfacing in my own mind. My daughter had posed the question in relation to the past. 'What was it like *then*?' was what she meant. 'What is it like now?' was the question that throbbed, faintly but insistently, at the back of my mind.

———

I arrive on a small commuter plane from Sydney via Dubbo. Apart from a brief stop in my hometown after my mother died in 1997, I had not been back in over thirty years. The 1997 visit was a very brief one, and I was too consumed with my mother's recent death as well as with a quick round of visits to her few remaining friends to take much in.

The weather is uncharacteristically cool for early February. The No-Frills Car Rental Company has not received the online car booking I made, but manages to find a small white Japanese thing that will do the job. On the short drive in from the airport to the city, I notice changes. The towering mountains of skimp—left over after the ore has been extracted—have largely disappeared. I later learn that they have been reprocessed. Just as noticeable is the absence of the mine poppet heads. These once dominated the skyline and were more emblematic of the town than anything else.

On a whim I had booked into the Mario's Palace hotel. Mario Celotto, the owner, now dead, had been a close friend of my father. His fifteen minutes of fame had come and gone with a guest appearance in *Priscilla, Queen of the Desert*, when his hotel was used for one of the film's locations. When I called and booked a room, the receptionist had said that the hotel was newly renovated. At least that's what I thought she'd said. I arrive to find the renovations, which were desperately overdue, have been put on hold.

The Palace was one of several grand hotels dotted along Argent Street. The exterior is still impressive, a solid three-story brick structure with a wide wrought-iron verandah on the second floor. Inside, a magnificent cedar staircase winds up to the second and third floors. The eccentric murals on the walls and ceiling are in good repair, but the rest of the place is falling apart. The burgundy carpet is stained and coming adrift at the seams. The floorboards creak as I cross the foyer to the stairs.

Upstairs, I find myself in a room next to the 'Priscilla Suite'. The rooms have evidently not been renovated since the 1950s. There on the bed is a maroon bedspread—an exact replica of the one that had adorned my own bed fifty years ago. The fittings, light switches, and bathroom are from the same era. Only the large flat screen television on the wall tells me that I have not been magically transported back to the middle of the preceding century.

I arrive without preconception or plan. My first thought is to find something to eat and drink. The front bar of the Palace Hotel (now renamed 'Mario's Palace Hotel') is closed —permanently, it would seem, and the side bar doesn't open until five. I walk a block to the Royal Exchange, another elegant hotel, and a favourite watering hole back in my student days. The elegant front façade has been replaced by a beauty salon, and a coffee shop occupies the space where the front bar used to be. I find a similar story at the other formerly grand hotels. Even those whose façades have survived have been transformed from watering holes for thirsty miners into boutiques, gift shops, and flea markets. One even houses a department of community welfare.

By the time I reach the end of the shopping strip, I begin to get the message. The fabled Silver City has lost its way. While not exactly on life support, it carries with it a tired, defeated air. There's no energy to the place. It's difficult to tell whether the few people ambling along the streets are local or tourists. Finally, I find something to eat —a hamburger, and not a bad one at that. My spirits lift a little, but I'm dispirited by the lack of energy. The town has been transformed from a raw, bustling mining town into a living museum. A few hundred people still work the mines, using new techniques that make it marginally profitable to mine low-grade ore, but it's a far cry from the thousands who once made the town one of the most profitable places on earth.

I return to my car and take a tour around town. My grandfather's house, built in the nineteenth century, is still standing, although it's barely visible under a tangle of trees and shrubs. The patch of ground at the front of the house that Katya's grandfather had toiled over is covered in weeds. The house where I was born and bred also remains standing, as does the Methodist Church on the opposite corner. Clearly, it is no longer used as a place of worship, or anything else as far as I can see, and is coming apart at the seams—and the car park is covered in weeds.

I'm staggered at the modesty of the hill at the end of the street; the towering hill with its killer road seems little more than a mound. The road has long since disappeared under saltbush and weeds, but the 'Road Closed' sign still stand incongruously at its base.

Bonnie's house is also there, looking exactly the same as it did almost fifty years ago. On a whim, I get out of the car and knock on the front door. I'm about to turn away when a young woman appears. Behind her a baby crawls in the hallway. She shakes her head. No, she knows no-one at all in the neighbourhood. Although she's been in the Hill for about four months, she rarely sees anyone in the street. 'It's a very quiet place', she says. 'I'm glad that we only have to be here for a couple of years. I can't wait to get back to Orange.'

I return to my car, and, on an impulse, drive out to Silverton, where I'd gone with Bonnie on the last day I ever saw her. Silverton was a substantial settlement in the days before the discovery twelve miles to the east of the largest deposits of silver, lead, and zinc on the earth. Now it was home to a handful of people. Visitors were drawn here by the fact that it had been the location for several movies, the best known being Mel Gibson's *Mad Max II*.

I wander around the Silverton Gaol, a rambling stone structure crammed with a random collection of rusting relics from leg irons to mining equipment, before repairing to the pub where I had experienced first-hand Bonnie's double life all those years ago. Apart from the fading photos of Mel Gibson that festoon the walls, the pub has not changed much. I'm disappointed that West End bitter is no longer available, and have to settle for a Pure Blonde. A handful of tourists push their way through the strips of plastic that are meant to repel flies and other insects. The Australians say 'G'day' and order beers. The foreigners take photos of the photos of Mel Gibson.

On the rear wall is a photo of the original Silverton Hotel, an impressive two-story stone structure that was destroyed by fire in 1919. My maternal grandmother had worked there as a chambermaid at the turn of the twentieth century. When we were kids, on Sunday afternoon drives that inevitably ended up in Silverton, we would climb like monkeys through the ruins of the old pub while our parents drank beer in its replacement. All traces of the original pub have gone now, and as I head back east, I wonder whether Broken Hill will end up like Silverton—next to nothing in the middle of nowhere.

Back in the Hill, I forage for food and drink. The most likely prospect is the Astra Hotel, which has more-or-less escaped the fate of most of the other grand drinking establishments. Upstairs, it's still a hotel. Downstairs, it has been transformed not into a boutique or souvenir shop but a wine bar and restaurant, and a rather elegant one at that. I sit at the end of the curved wooden bar and order a glass of sauvignon blanc, which comes in a generously sized glass.

Apart from a middle-aged couple drinking champagne in the corner, the bar is empty. The plump, pretty barmaid, who announces herself as Maddie, is on for a chat. By the time I'm ready for a refill, I have Maddie's life story. Originally from Newcastle, she came to Broken Hill with her family at the age of eleven. She and her partner have a young son. 'Broken Hill is the perfect place for us', she tells me. 'It's cheap and it's safe. When I go shopping, I leave the house unlocked, and I can leave my keys in the car. I've worked in this bar for three years, and in that time I've only ever seen two fights. And I think that was between people who were from out of town.'

What a contrast with the past, when there was a fight on every corner. People went looking for fights. Alcohol and the harshness and frustrations of life saw to that. Accidentally catching someone's eye was provocation enough to earn a fist in the ear.

Maddie has vague plans of going to Sydney to do a degree in nursing, but would then return to Broken Hill. There are no education opportunities her, nothing for young people at all. It's all because of the City Council. They don't want to encourage people, particularly young people. 'It's not that they're killing the town', she says. 'They're just letting it die of its own accord.'

I have a seared kangaroo fillet with mustard mashed potatoes and a glass of red wine. It's excellent—a dish that any trendy city bistro would be happy to serve. The days when fine dining began and ended with an overcooked sirloin at the Royal Exchange have well and truly gone. So not all about the place is in decay. At the end of the meal, Maddie gives me the rest of the bottle of wine in a plastic bag. 'You might want a nightcap', she says.

Back at the Palace Hotel, a private party is in full swing on the verandah. Although the beer and wine flow freely, the group is of good cheer. I settle myself into a corner table and finish off my bottle of wine. One or two people nod affably as they pass by. Maddie is right. Gone is the aggression that was a hallmark of social life way back then.

The following day, I roam the Central Business District, such as it is. The corner block where Rupert's newspaper office had once stood is now a car park. Astonishingly, however, the union newspaper, *The Barrier Daily Truth,* is still being printed and looks much the same as it did forty years ago. Hardly any of the establishments that I remember from my youth remain. Dryen's the menswear store, scene of numerous humiliations is gone. Torpy's shoe-store, that had once been managed by my Uncle Dave, no longer sits squarely in the centre of the block. Bon Marche is a distant memory, as is Frank Griffs, Johnny's Snack Bar, where you could get the juiciest hamburgers in town, and Bunny Maloney's Barber Shop, where I once got a clop over the ears for demanding a Hollywood cut.

All that remains, to remind me that this is, indeed, the town where I grew up, is the row of fine buildings sitting squarely in the central block—the War Memorial, the Courthouse where my grandfather stood trial for attempted murder, the technical college, the police station, the town hall and the post office. All fine buildings, reminders of the wealth that had one characterised the town. Although, even here, all is not as it seems. On closer inspection, I see that the Town Hall, the finest building of them all, is but a façade. The building behind the façade has been demolished and replaced with yet another car park.

My last day in the Hill dawns clear, bright and uncharacteristically crisp for this time of year. Yesterday I decided that I needed to go down one of the mines to bring closure to my trip. The tourist brochure that I picked up yesterday lists a trip underground as a 'must'; however, the young woman at the hotel reception says the only mine offering underground tours is the Daydream Mine out on the Silverton Road. Having already been to Silverton, I have to retrace my path, something I'm loath to do.

I went underground once when I was a schoolboy. I was under the legal age for going underground, but my Uncle Don, who was a mine manager, arranged it. The experience left an indelible impression. The deeper into the earth you go, the hotter it gets, and in the belly of the mine refrigerated air had to be pumped into the shafts in order to make working conditions bearable. The old workings, where my grandfather had extracted ore with pick and shovel, were only waist high. In addition to enduring the heat and the lung-corroding dust, the miners had to hew the earth bent double. The broken ore was hauled along the main drives by draught horses. These horses would spend all week in the pits, because it took hours to roll them onto their backs and bring them to the surface.

The dirt road leading to the Daydream Mine runs due east just short of Silverton. At the junction, a temporary sign reads 'Daydream Mine Road Closed.' A week before, four inches of rain had fallen in the district. However, things now seemed reasonably dry, so I decide to take a risk.

The road is corrugated in parts and covered in layers of fine cracker-dust in others. Here and there, deep ruts have been carved into the road by flash floods. It is a bone-jarring ride in my little Japanese rental car. I come to a creek that is still flowing across the road and would have turned back but for the fact that there is nowhere to turn. I ease the car forward and make it through the water. It almost stalls as I gun the engine in order to get it up the steep incline on the other side. A little further on I hit a deep sand drift, and go into a four-wheel slide. I manage to correct the car and continue on, although my heart is pounding. Getting stuck here wouldn't do at all. Not on this road. Not on this day. I had none of the basic equipment to free myself, not even a shovel. Even out here in the bush, hire car companies assume that their clients have more sense than to get off the beaten track.

After what seems an eternity, I come to the boundary of the Daydream Mine property. I let myself through the gate and proceed towards the mine, relieved to have made it. However, about 100 metres from the gate, the rutted road dips sharply to the right. Luckily, the bend forces me to slow down. Had I been traveling at normal speed, I would have driven straight into another creek bed. Unlike the previous creek that I traversed, which had a gentle decline and a somewhat steeper incline, this one is quite precipitous. I bring the car to a complete stop and check it out.

There is no water, but at the bottom is what look like a deep drift of river sand. I'm caught in a quandary. Having come this far, I'm loath to turn back. However, I recall several incidents from my youth earlier adulthood in which I had become stuck for hours in the desert until being rescued. If the drift of sand is deep enough, your wheels begin to spin, digging the car ever deeper into the sand. On more than one occasion, I ended up with the belly of the car resting on the sand, stuck fast until someone with a four-wheel drive and tow-rope happened along to pull me out. One time, I was stuck for over five hours, and on another occasion when I was out shooting rabbits a couple of friends, we got bogged in the soft red sand on the edge of a dam and there we stayed for the rest of the night.

Given that I'm booked to fly out later that afternoon, it seems the height of folly to press on. Reluctantly, I back and fill the car and make my way back to the bitumen. On the outskirts of town, there is a sign pointing up a side street: 'White's Mineral Art and Living Mining Museum.' In my experience, these folksy little museums are usually pretty cheesy and hardly worth the entrance money. However, now that my plans to go down the mine have been thwarted, I have the rest of the morning to kill. On a whim, I turned down a side street and soon find myself drawing up in front of an extremely cheesy-looking museum.

Inside, however, the museum turns out to be anything but cheesy. Created and run by Kevin 'Bushy' White, a former miner, the museum replicates an underground mining drive. Although wandering around the museum is a very different experience from going underground in a real working mine, it is nevertheless a fascinating experience. Bushy has gathered together mining implements and artefacts that tell the history of underground mining in Broken Hill and elsewhere.

Particularly fascinating, are the 'paintings' created by Bushy from finely crushed minerals of many different hues. These works of art showing historical buildings around town as well as scenes from the mines should have been pure kitsch. However, they are so well executed that they really are works of art. Bushy is a quintessential Broken Hillite—unassuming and down to earth, he creates his works of art out of love. If you want to purchase one, that's fine. If you don't, that's fine too.

When I announced to Bushy that I'm a prodigal son returning, however briefly, to The Hill, and have in fact been underground, he warms to me and we reminisce about the Broken Hill I have returned to after all these years. My Broken Hill no longer exists, but its ghost can be glimpsed in Bushy's mine. I buy a little book containing reproductions of some of Bushy's artwork, which he autographs for me, and take my leave.

———

What an extraordinary thing it is to fall in love with someone or something you have known all your life. At one arresting moment, your focus shifts dramatically, something falls into place, and you see the person or the place as if for the first time.

Some days after my trip to The Hill, I'm flying from Sydney back to Hong Kong, my adopted home. My preferred overnight flight is cancelled, and I am consigned to a day flight. Pure torture. Small children with sharp teeth. Movies that at street level I wouldn't cross the street to watch. Struggling with *The Financial Times*, almost unreadable in the twilight zone of the cabin. (What genius had the bright idea of printing it on pink paper?)

Then it comes to me. Tom Eliot's words from *Little Gidding*, if I remember right.

> *We shall not cease from exploration*
> *And the end of all our exploring*
> *Will be to arrive where we started*
> *And know the place for the first time.*

To the aggravation of the otherwise kindly gentleman sitting next to me, I raise the shade. And fall in love. Eliot's *Little Gidding* piece has done it. Reverberating down the years. Down those old dusty streets where I was first seduced by his surrealistic imagery—doling out our lives in coffee spoons, whimpering ends to the world, patients anaesthetised and all the rest of it. Here below me is My Country. At 35,000 feet.

Last night, before I flew out, I watched a television program called *Who Do You Think You Are?*, which picks some celebrity and traces his or her roots. This program happened to be all about one of my sporting heroes, Michael O'Loughlin—recently retired from my beloved Sydney Swans football team. In the piece, Mick traced his ancestry to an aboriginal community in the Coorong in South Australia. It was intensely moving because he found his piece of earth.

I have no piece of earth that I can claim as my birthright. Indigenous Australians have inhabited the wide brown land over which I fly for longer than time itself. In some ways, I envy O'Loughlin. Finding his spiritual roots clearly moved him dearly. In other ways, I don't really care. Like Mick, I had no choice where or when I was born. I've spent the majority of my life as a stranger in strange lands.

But seeing the wrinkled walnut skin of Australia as I fly out of it yet again, in daylight this time, I realise where I want my bones to end up.

GLOSSARY OF AUSTRALIAN TERMS

This glossary provides a 'translation' from Australian English to American English of some of the words that may be unfamiliar to readers in North America.

- arse-over-tit: head-over-heels
- arse: ass (rear end)
- arvo: afternoon
- billy cart: a go-cart
- biscuits: cookies
- bitumen: asphalt
- bushie: a person who lives in the Outback (the "Bush")
- chook: a chicken
- claypan: a dense, compact, layer in the subsoil with a much higher clay content than the layer on top, from which it is separated by a sharply defined boundary. A claypan is hard when dry and sticky when wet. It limits or slows the downward movement of water through the soil.

- dingo: a wild Australian dog
- dipso: a dipsomaniac; i.e., a drunkard
- Duco: A brand name assigned to a product line of automotive lacquer developed by the DuPont Company in the 1920s.
- dunny: outhouse (outdoor toilet)
- esky: an ice chest (from "Eskimo," a brand of ice chest)
- euro: a wallaroo (marsupial animal similar to a kangaroo)
- fag: a cigarette; a homosexual
- Feltex: a brand of carpet
- gaol: a jail
- ghost gum (tree): a species of eucalyptus tree with white bark
- gum (tree): a eucalyptus tree
- jinker: a truck used for transporting logs and timber
- jumper: sweater
- lippy: disrespectful
- mate: friend
- milko: a milkman (milk delivery person)
- nick: to steal
- paddy wagon: a police vehicle used to transport criminals
- pasty (plural: pasties): pastry dough filled with vegetables and meat
- pensioner: a retired person, who lives off a government pension
- Pom: a citizen of Great Britain (an uncomplimentary term)
- poof, poofter: a male homosexual

- rabbito: a person who traps and sells rabbits
- spanner: a wrench
- spider: an ice cream float (ice cream in soda)
- spinifex: a type of Australian grass with stiff, sharp leaves that grows in clumps, specially in sand.
- stope: A part of a mine shaped like steps, from where minerals are being extracted. The step shape allows access to steep hillsides.
- stubby: a smaller-sized, short, squat bottle of beer
- trainers: sneakers; athletic shoes
- ute: pickup truck (from "utility truck")
- wag school: to skip school

ABOUT THE AUTHOR

David Nunan (born 11 October 1949 in Broken Hill, Australia) is an Australian linguist who has focused on the teaching of English. His ELT textbook series *Go For It!* is the largest selling textbook series in the world, with sales exceeding 2.5 billion copies.

Nunan began his career in Teaching English as a Second Language (ESL) in Sydney, Australia, before completing graduate studies in the United Kingdom. He has worked as a teacher, researcher, and consultant in many countries including Australia, the United Kingdom, the United States, Thailand, Singapore, Japan, Hong Kong, and a number of Latin American countries.

Nunan's academic and student textbooks are published by Cambridge University Press, Oxford University Press, Anaheim University Press, Palgrave/Macmillan, and the EFL publishing division of Cengage Learning. Nunan is Vice-President for Academic Affairs at Anaheim University based in Anaheim, California. Nunan serves in a concurrent role as Dean of the Graduate School of Education and Professor of Teaching English to Speakers of Other Languages (TESOL) at Anaheim University, where he has worked since 1996.

In 2000, Nunan served as President of TESOL Inc., the world's largest language teaching association, and was the first person to serve as President from outside North America. Previously Nunan served as Chair and Professor of Applied Linguistics at the University of Hong Kong and has been involved in the teaching of graduate programs for such institutions as the University of Hawaii, Monterey Institute for International Studies, Sophia University, Chulalongkorn University, Thailand and many others. He is Academic Advisor to the GlobalEnglish Corporation, and is on the Executive Committee of The International Research Foundation for English Language Education.

In 2002 Nunan received a congressional citation from the United States House of Representatives for his services to English language education through his pioneering work in online education through Anaheim University. In 2003 he was ranked the 7th most influential Australian in Asia by Business Review Weekly, and in 2005 he was named one of the top "50 Australians who Matter." In November 2006, Nunan was awarded the Convocation medal for outstanding achievement and contribution internationally to the profession of teaching English as a second language from Flinders University, where he earned his Ph.D. in Education and Linguistics. In December 2006, Nunan was invited by the Australian Prime Minister to attend the Advance Leading 100 Global Australians Summit in Sydney, Australia.